Letts
gets you through

C000080700

KS2
ARITHMETIC
SATs SUCCESS
WORKBOOK

Ages 8–9

KS2
ARITHMETIC
SATs
WORKBOOK

PAUL BROADBENT

# About this book

## Mental arithmetic

Mental arithmetic involves carrying out calculations and working with numbers in your head, without the help of a calculator or computer. It is an important part of your child's education in maths and will help them to manage everyday situations in later life. This book will help your child to solve increasingly difficult problems in their head and at greater speed. It provides the opportunity to learn, practise and check progress in a wide range of mental arithmetic skills, such as addition, subtraction, multiplication, division and working with fractions, decimals and measures. This book will also aid preparation for the **Key Stage 2 mathematics** test.

## Features of the book

*Learn and revise* – explains and refreshes mental arithmetic skills and strategies.

*Practice activities* – a variety of tasks to see how well your child has grasped each skill.

*Mental arithmetic tests* – 20 questions which test and reinforce your child's understanding of the preceding topics.

*Speed tests* and *Progress charts* – the one-minute tests challenge your child to carry out mental calculations at increasing speed and the progress charts enable them to record their results.

*Key facts* – a summary of key points that your child should learn by heart and memorise.

*Answers* are in a pull-out booklet at the centre of the book.

## Mental arithmetic tips

- Cooking with your child provides opportunities to use measures – reading scales, converting between units and calculating with amounts.

- Look at prices and compare amounts when shopping. Use receipts to find differences between prices.

- Play board games, such as a simplified version of *Monopoly*, and dice games, such as *Yahtzee*, taking opportunities to add and subtract numbers and money.

- Addition and subtraction facts to 20 and the multiplication tables are basic key facts that your child will need to know so that they can solve problems with bigger numbers. Regularly practise these facts – you could write them on sticky notes around the house for your child to see or answer.

- Short, regular practice to build confidence is better than spending too long on an activity so that boredom creeps in. Keep each session to 20–30 minutes.

# Contents

# Counting and numbers

Counting patterns can use steps of different numbers. To work out the steps, look at the difference between the numbers.

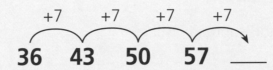

This is going up in sevens. The next number is 64.

When you count backwards past zero you will use negative numbers. Picture them on a number line to help you see them in sequence.

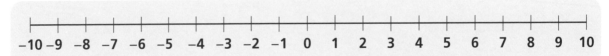

## Practice activities

1. Write the missing numbers in each sequence.

   a)  12      18      ____      30      ____      42      ____

   b)  ____    ____    100     125     150     ____    200

   c)  27      ____    45      54      ____    ____    81

   d)  7       14      21      ____    ____    ____    49

   e)  2000    3000    ____    ____    ____    7000    8000

2. Write the next two numbers in each of these.

   a)  106     101     96      91      86      ____    ____

   b)  71      74      77      80      83      ____    ____

   c)  83      77      71      65      59      ____    ____

   d)  230     280     330     380     430     ____    ____

   e)  169     167     165     163     161     ____    ____

**3.** Write the missing numbers on each number line.

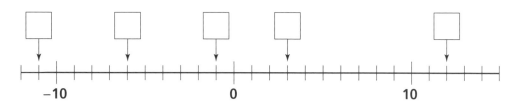

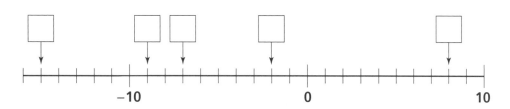

**4.** This is the halfway number between 588 and 596.

588 ------ 592 ------ 596

What are these halfway numbers?

a) 580 ------ _____ ------ 620

b) 945 ------ _____ ------ 961

c) 422 ------ _____ ------ 482

d) 678 ------ _____ ------ 700

**5.** Count in these steps. Write the missing numbers.

a) Count in 10s   → 972 _____ _____ _____ 1012

b) Count in 10s   → 4000 _____ _____ _____ 4040

c) Count in 100s  → 859 _____ _____ _____ 1259

d) Count in 100s  → 6923 _____ _____ _____ 7323

e) Count in 1000s → 519 _____ _____ _____ 4519

f) Count in 1000s → 6795 _____ _____ _____ 10 795

# Place value

## Learn and revise

Look at this number and how it is made:

**4183 = 4000 + 100 + 80 + 3**

**four thousand one hundred and eighty-three**

| Thousands | Hundreds | Tens | Ones |
|-----------|----------|------|------|
| 4 | 1 | 8 | 3 |

4000 > 100 > 80 > 3

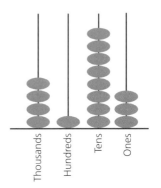

## Practice activities

1. Write the missing numbers.

   a) 4612 → 4000 + 600 + _____ + _____

   b) 1498 → _____ + _____ + 90 + 8

   c) 2753 → 2000 + _____ + 50 + _____

   d) 6849 → _____ + _____ + _____ + 9

   e) 8147 → _____ + 100 + _____ + _____

2. Write these as numbers.

   a) four thousand five hundred and thirty-two _____

   b) one thousand and twenty-six _____

   c) six thousand seven hundred and three _____

   d) seven thousand five hundred and ninety-nine _____

**3.** What numbers do each of these arrow cards show?

a) 6000 > 500 > 20 > 8 > _____

b) 1000 > 900 > 80 > 5 > _____

c) 5000 > 700 > 30 > 1 > _____

**4. a)** What number is 2000 more than 1345? _____

**b)** What number is 400 more than 6356? _____

**c)** What number is 4000 less than 9251? _____

**d)** What number is 80 less than 5083? _____

**5.** Write the numbers shown by each abacus.

a)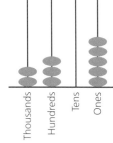

_____

b)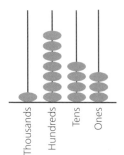

_____

c)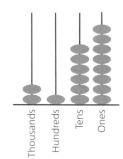

_____

**6.** Draw five beads on each abacus to make two different numbers greater than 1000. Write each number in words and numerals.

a)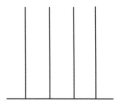

_____

_____

_____

b)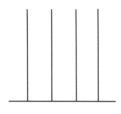

_____

_____

_____

# Comparing and ordering numbers

Remember that < and > are used to compare numbers.

| | |
|---|---|
| **< means 'is less than'** | **> means 'is greater than'** |
| 1439 < 1827 | 4503 > 4305 |
| 1439 is less than 1827 | 4503 is greater than 4305 |

When you compare numbers to put them in order, you must look carefully at the value of the digits.

If you have a list of numbers to put in order, look at the place value of the digits, starting with the thousands.

**Example:** Put these in order, starting with the smallest.

2345   4630   2092   2354   1785   ⟶   1785   2092   2345   2354   4630

## Practice activities

1. Write < or > to make these correct.

   a)  4065 _____ 4550          b)  5633 _____ 5363

   c)  2703 _____ 2699          d)  4185 _____ 4850

2. Underline the smallest number in this set. Draw a circle around the largest.

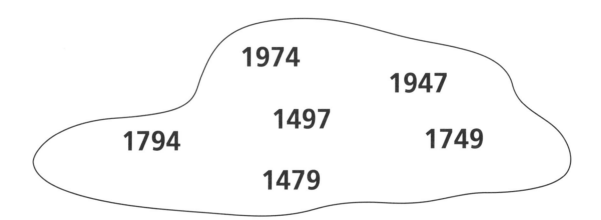

1974

1947

1497

1749

1794

1479

8

# Comparing and ordering numbers

**3.** Write each set of numbers in order of size, starting with the smallest.

a)

| 3149 | 3150 |
|------|------|
| 2087 | 2900 |

_____ _____ _____ _____
smallest

b)

| 6102 | 5904 |
|------|------|
| 5933 | 6244 |

_____ _____ _____ _____
smallest

c)

| 8003 | 8030 |
|------|------|
| 8300 | 8303 |

_____ _____ _____ _____
smallest

d)

| 9213 | 8959 |
|------|------|
| 8599 | 9132 |

_____ _____ _____ _____
smallest

**4.** These are the heights of some of the tallest mountains around the world. Write them in height order starting with the tallest mountain.

Aconcagua  6960 m          K2 8611 m

Chappal Waddi  2409 m    Kilimanjaro  5893 m

Cook  3766 m                   Lenin Peak  7134 m

Everest  8848 m               McKinley  6194 m

| Name of mountain | Height (m) |
|------------------|------------|
|                  |            |
|                  |            |
|                  |            |
|                  |            |
|                  |            |
|                  |            |
|                  |            |
|                  |            |

# Mental arithmetic test 1

**1.** Write the number at each arrow.

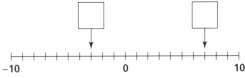

**2.** Write the missing numbers.

5732 ⟶ 5000 + _____ + _____ + 2

**3.** Write the missing numbers in this sequence.

400   350   _____   _____   200

**4.** What number is 300 more than 1176?

_____

**5.** Write the next two numbers.

182   177   172   _____   _____

**6.** Write these numbers in order, starting with the smallest.

1956   1596   1965

_____   _____   _____

**7.** Write the number on this abacus.

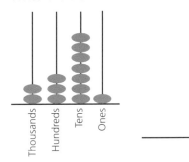

_____

**8.** What is the halfway number?

380 ------ _____ ------ 440

**9.** Count in 10s and write the missing numbers.

3430   _____   _____   3460

**10.** Underline the smallest number and circle the largest number.

6574    5674    5476    6745    7456

**11.** What is the halfway number?

218 ------ _____ ------ 242

**12.** Write the missing numbers in this sequence.

28   _____   36   40   _____

**13.** Count in 100s and write the missing numbers.

882   _____   _____   1182

**14.** Write eight thousand nine hundred and fifteen in numbers.

_____

**15.** Write the number.

8000 + 300 + 50 + 1 ⟶ _____

**16.** Circle the number that is 1000 more than 5701.

5801        5711
    6701        6570

**17.** Write the number at each arrow.

**18.** Write the next two numbers.

88   92   96   _____   _____

**19.** Write < or > to make these correct.

6060 _____ 6006    5195 _____ 5915

**20.** What number is 5000 less than 9470?

_____

Score        /20

10

# Mental arithmetic test 2

1. Count in 100s and write the missing numbers.

   1904 _____ _____ 2204

2. Write two thousand four hundred and fifty-six as a number.

   _____

3. What is the halfway number?

   175 ------ _____ ------ 235

4. Write the next two numbers.

   170   190   210   _____   _____

5. What number is 70 less than 1492?

   _____

6. Write < or > to make these correct.

   4930 _____ 9390   2715 _____ 2175

7. Write these numbers in order, starting with the smallest.

   8787      7887      8877

   _____   _____   _____

8. Write the number on this abacus.

   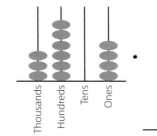

   _____

9. Write the number at each arrow.

   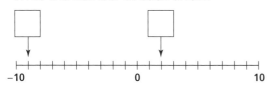

10. Write the missing numbers in this sequence.

    _____   40   48   _____   64

11. Write the next two numbers.

    22   25   28   _____   _____

12. Write the number at each arrow.

    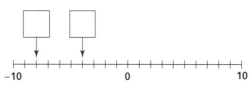

13. Write the missing numbers.

    9418 ⟶ _____ + 400 + _____ + 8

14. What number is 50 more than 1270?

    _____

15. Underline the smallest number and circle the largest number.

    3291    3092    3902    3910    3309

16. Count in 1000s and write the missing numbers.

    790 _____ _____ 3790

17. Write the missing numbers in this sequence.

    632   532   _____   332   _____

18. What is the halfway number?

    683 ------ _____ ------ 691

19. Write the number.

    4000 + 700 + 20 + 8 ⟶ _____

20. Circle the number that is 10 more than 1190.

    2000        1100        1200        2100

# Addition and subtraction facts

## Learn and revise

Addition and subtraction are connected. Use any facts you know to help learn others.

Do you know that $8 + 3 = 11$?

You can use this to work out these facts:

$3 + 8 = 11$                    $11 - 8 = 3$                    $11 - 3 = 8$

Remember that subtraction is the inverse, or opposite, of addition.

## Practice activities

1. Write the missing numbers in this addition grid. Colour the facts you know instantly and then learn the others.

| + | 1 | 2 | 3 | 4 | 5 | 6 | 7 | 8 | 9 | 10 |
|---|---|---|---|---|---|---|---|---|---|----|
| 1 | 2 | 3 | | | | | | | | |
| 2 | 3 | 4 | | | | | | | | |
| 3 | | | 6 | | | | | | | |
| 4 | | | | | | | | | | |
| 5 | | | | | | | | | | |
| 6 | | | | | | | | | | |
| 7 | | | | | | | | | | |
| 8 | | | | | | | | | | |
| 9 | | | | | | | | | | |
| 10 | | | | | | | | | | |

# Addition and subtraction facts

**2.** Write the missing numbers in these trios.
The top number is the sum of the two numbers below.

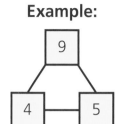

**a)**
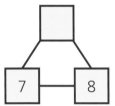

**b)**
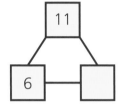

**c)**
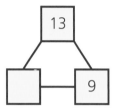

**d)**
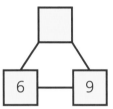

**e)**
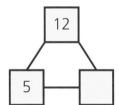

**f)**
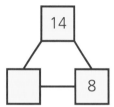

**3.** Write the missing numbers on these addition walls.
The top number is the sum of the two numbers below.

**Example:**

**a)**
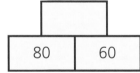

**b)**
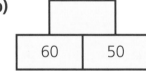

**c)**
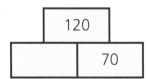

**d)**
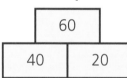

**e)**
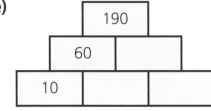

**f)**
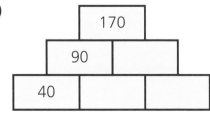

# Addition

## Learn and revise

Break numbers up so that you can add them in your head.

**Example:** What is 63 add 18?

$63 + \textbf{18}$ =

$63 + \textbf{10} + \textbf{8}$ =

$73 + 8$ =

$\textbf{70} + \textbf{3} + 8$ = $70 + 11 = 81$

Hold the bigger number in your head and break up the smaller number.

**Example:** Add together 273 and 40.

$\textbf{273} + 40$ =

$\textbf{200} + \textbf{70} + \textbf{3} + 40$ =

$\textbf{200} + \textbf{70} + 40 + \textbf{3}$ =

$200 + 110 + 3$ = $313$

Add the hundreds and tens and then add on the ones.

## Practice activities

1.  Add these mentally and write the answers.

    a)  $77 + 5$  = _____

    b)  $58 + 9$  = _____

    c)  $35 + 8$  = _____

    d)  $86 + 7$  = _____

    e)  $58 + 13$  = _____

    f)  $47 + 25$  = _____

    g)  $39 + 32$  = _____

    h)  $68 + 19$  = _____

2.  Now add these mentally and write the answers.

    a)  $71 + 60$  = _____

    b)  $64 + 50$  = _____

    c)  $85 + 30$  = _____

    d)  $68 + 40$  = _____

    e)  $384 + 40$ = _____

    f)  $257 + 60$ = _____

    g)  $191 + 70$ = _____

    h)  $239 + 80$ = _____

**3.** Complete these addition grids.

**a)**

| + | 80 | 60 | 90 | 70 |
|---|----|----|----|----|
| **253** | 333 | | | |
| **185** | | | | |
| **693** | | | | |

**b)**

| + | 45 | 38 | 52 | 27 |
|---|----|----|----|----|
| **35** | 80 | | | |
| **26** | | | | |
| **41** | | | | |

**4.** Write the missing digits 0–6 in these additions.

**0**   **2**   **4**   **6**

**1**   **3**   **5**

$45 + \boxed{\phantom{0}}\,8 = 83$   $\boxed{\phantom{0}}\,6 + 14 = 7\boxed{\phantom{0}}$

$19 + 4\boxed{\phantom{0}} = \boxed{\phantom{0}}\,3$   $\boxed{\phantom{0}}\,7 + 35 = 5\boxed{\phantom{0}}$

**5.** I am thinking of a number. If I add 60 to my number, I end up with double the number I started with. What number was I thinking of?

_____

# Subtraction

## Learn and revise

There are different strategies you can use to subtract mentally.

Counting on from the smallest number is a good method.

**Example:** What is 45 subtract 18?

Count on from 18 to 20 and then to 45.

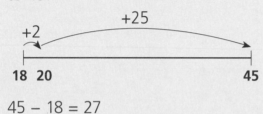

$45 - 18 = 27$

You could try breaking numbers up so that you can subtract them in your head.

**Example:** Take away 80 from 135.

$$135 - 80 =$$
$$130 + 5 - 80 =$$
$$130 - 80 = 50 + 5 = 55$$

Subtract the hundreds and tens and then add on the ones.

## Practice activities

1. Use the number lines to help you subtract these mentally.

a)

```
├──────────────┤
19            56
```

$56 - 19 =$ _____

b)

```
├──────────────┤
27            43
```

$43 - 27 =$ _____

c)

```
├──────────────┤
52            91
```

$91 - 52 =$ _____

d)

```
├──────────────┤
38            85
```

$85 - 38 =$ _____

e)

```
├──────────────┤
35            64
```

$64 - 35 =$ _____

f)

```
├──────────────┤
56            74
```

$74 - 56 =$ _____

**2.** Answer these.

**a)** Take 60 away from 155.  _____

**b)** Subtract 40 from 118.  _____

**c)** What is 70 less than 142?  _____

**d)** Take away 90 from 161.  _____

**e)** What is 128 take away 50?  _____

**3.** Complete each chart with the numbers coming out of each subtraction machine.

**a)** IN → ⟨–70⟩ → OUT

| IN | 155 | 163 | 105 | 132 | 111 | 149 |
|---|---|---|---|---|---|---|
| OUT | 85 | | | | | |

**b)** IN → ⟨–250⟩ → OUT

| IN | 300 | 900 | 400 | 700 | 800 | 600 |
|---|---|---|---|---|---|---|
| OUT | 50 | | | | | |

**4.** Look at the heights of these sunflowers and answer these questions.

**a)** How much taller is Sunflower A than Sunflower B? _____ cm

**b)** How much taller is Sunflower B than Sunflower C? _____ cm

**c)** If Sunflower D grows to be the same height as Sunflower A, how many more centimetres will it need to grow? _____ cm

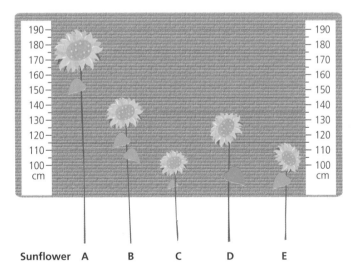

**d)** What is the difference in height between Sunflower D and Sunflower E? _____ cm

**e)** How much shorter is Sunflower E than Sunflower B? _____ cm

# Mental arithmetic test 3

1. 150 – 70 = \_\_\_\_

2. What is the total of 26 and 35?

   \_\_\_\_

3. 40 + \_\_\_\_ = 120

4. 491 + 30 = \_\_\_\_

5. What number is 200 less than 818?

   \_\_\_\_

6. 110 – \_\_\_\_ = 30

7. I am thinking of a number. If I subtract 60, I am left with 95. What is my number?

   \_\_\_\_

8. 47 + 9 = \_\_\_\_

9. Subtract 150 from each of these.

   400   \_\_\_\_

   700   \_\_\_\_

10. 52 – 19 = \_\_\_\_

11. 143 – 90 = \_\_\_\_

12. 5 + \_\_\_\_ = 13

13. 28 + 58 = \_\_\_\_

14. 63 – 14 = \_\_\_\_

15. Add 30 to each of these.

    491   \_\_\_\_

    207   \_\_\_\_

16. \_\_\_\_ – 70 = 56

17. 53 + 28 = \_\_\_\_

18. Complete this addition wall. The top number is the sum of the two numbers below.

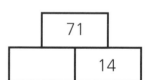

19. 159 – \_\_\_\_ = 60

20. What number is 7 more than 55?

    \_\_\_\_

Score      /20

18

# Mental arithmetic test 4

1.  135 − 60 = _____

2.  Two parcels weigh 47 kg each. What is their total weight?

    _____ kg

3.  56 + 8 = _____

4.  90 + 221 = _____

5.  Take away 500 from 785.

    _____

6.  _____ + 9 = 17

7.  330 − _____ = 50

8.  Complete this addition wall. The top number is the sum of the two numbers below.

    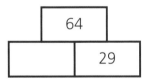

9.  84 + 30 = _____

10. 90 + _____ = 180

11. Add 70 to each of these.

    140    _____

    96    _____

12. 375 + 50 = _____

13. 48 + 36 = _____

14. A jug holds 600 ml of milk and 250 ml is poured out. How much milk is left?

    _____ ml

15. 220 − _____ = 90

16. 70 + 482 = _____

17. Subtract 40 from each of these.

    507    _____

    316    _____

18. _____ − 8 = 195

19. 60 − 34 = _____

20. I am thinking of a number. If I subtract 8, my answer is 29. What is my number?

    _____

Score    /20

# Multiplication and division facts

## Learn and revise

The 11 times table has an interesting pattern. Learn these facts.

| | |
|---|---|
| 11 × 1 = 11 | 11 × 7 = 77 |
| 11 × 2 = 22 | 11 × 8 = 88 |
| 11 × 3 = 33 | 11 × 9 = 99 |
| 11 × 4 = 44 | 11 × 10 = 110 |
| 11 × 5 = 55 | 11 × 11 = 121 |
| 11 × 6 = 66 | 11 × 12 = 132 |

The 12 times table is double the 6 times table. You could also learn it by multiplying by 10 and then by 2.

**Example:**

12 × 7 ⟶ (10 × 7) + (2 × 7) = 84

| | |
|---|---|
| 12 × 1 = 12 | 12 × 7 = 84 |
| 12 × 2 = 24 | 12 × 8 = 96 |
| 12 × 3 = 36 | 12 × 9 = 108 |
| 12 × 4 = 48 | 12 × 10 = 120 |
| 12 × 5 = 60 | 12 × 11 = 132 |
| 12 × 6 = 72 | 12 × 12 = 144 |

## Practice activities

**1.** Write the multiplication and division facts for these numbers.

**Example:**

④ ⑥ ㉔

4 × 6 = 24

6 × 4 = 24

24 ÷ 4 = 6

24 ÷ 6 = 4

**a)** ⑦ ㉟ ⑤

____ × ____ = ____

____ × ____ = ____

____ ÷ ____ = ____

____ ÷ ____ = ____

**b)** ⑥ ⑦ ㊷

____ × ____ = ____

____ × ____ = ____

____ ÷ ____ = ____

____ ÷ ____ = ____

**c)** ⑨ ④ ㊱

____ × ____ = ____

____ × ____ = ____

____ ÷ ____ = ____

____ ÷ ____ = ____

**d)** ⑧ ⑥ ㊽

____ × ____ = ____

____ × ____ = ____

____ ÷ ____ = ____

____ ÷ ____ = ____

**e)** ⑬⑫ ⑪ ⑫

____ × ____ = ____

____ × ____ = ____

____ ÷ ____ = ____

____ ÷ ____ = ____

# Multiplication and division facts

**2.** Write the missing numbers in these multiplication triangles. The top number is the product of the two numbers below.

**a)**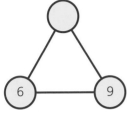

**b)**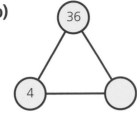

**c)**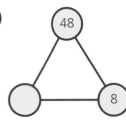

**d)**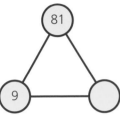

**e)**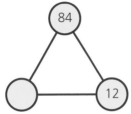

**f)**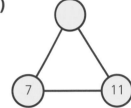

**3.** Use doubling to answer these.

**a)**
3 × 3 = 9
6 × 3 = 18
12 × 3 = ____

**b)**
3 × 5 = ____
6 × 5 = ____
12 × 5 = ____

**c)**
3 × 8 = ____
6 × 8 = ____
12 × 8 = ____

**d)**
3 × 4 = ____
6 × 4 = ____
12 × 4 = ____

**e)**
3 × 9 = ____
6 × 9 = ____
12 × 9 = ____

**f)**
3 × 7 = ____
6 × 7 = ____
12 × 7 = ____

**4.** Complete these. Circle those you know instantly.

8 × 11 = ____          4 × 7 = ____          3 × 9 = ____          7 × 6 = ____

12 × 6 = ____          11 × 2 = ____          9 × 4 = ____          10 × 8 = ____

7 × 3 = ____          9 × 2 = ____          6 × 3 = ____          11 × 11 = ____

5 × 12 = ____          8 × 7 = ____          9 × 9 = ____          6 × 8 = ____

**5.** What's my number? Work out the mystery number for each of these.

**a)** When I divide my number by 7, the answer is 8.          ____

**b)** When I multiply my number by 6, the answer is 42.          ____

**c)** When I divide my number by 3 and then add 5, the answer is 12.          ____

**d)** When I multiply my number by 5 and then subtract 6, the answer is 39.          ____

# Multiplication

## Learn and revise

Use the tables facts that you know to help you multiply bigger numbers.

3 × 5 = 15

300 × 5 = 1500

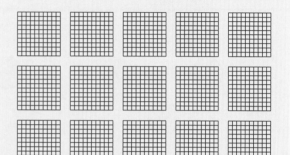

Try using factor pairs to help multiply larger numbers.

**Example:** What is 35 × 8?

Break the numbers up into factor pairs:

5 and 7 are factors of 35          2 and 4 are factors of 8

5 × 7 × 2 × 4 ◄——————— *Rearrange the factors to make them easier to multiply.*

5 × 2 × 7 × 4 = 10 × 28

So 35 × 8 = 280

## Practice activities

1. Answer these.

   a)  4 × 9 = _____   b)  6 × 8 = _____   c)  8 × 7 = _____

       400 × 9 = _____       600 × 8 = _____       800 × 7 = _____

   d)  9 × 3 = _____   e)  7 × 7 = _____   f)  4 × 12 = _____

       900 × 3 = _____       700 × 7 = _____       400 × 12 = _____

2. Complete this multiplication grid.

| × | 30 | 60 | 80 |
|---|----|----|----|
| 20 | 600 | | |
| 90 | | | |
| 40 | | | |

**3.** The two bottom numbers on each triangle are multiplied to give the top number. Write the missing numbers on these triangles.

a)
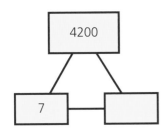

b)
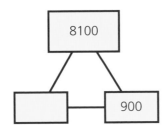

c)
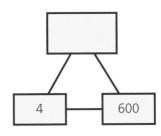

d)
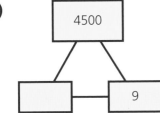

e)
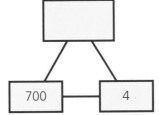

f)
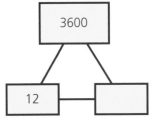

**4.** Multiply these sets of three numbers. Look for pairs to multiply first.

a)
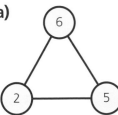

_____

b)
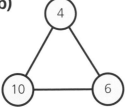

_____

c)
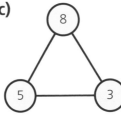

_____

d)
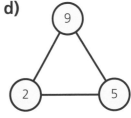

_____

**5.** Look for factor pairs to answer these.

a) **25 × 4**          Factors of 25: ____, ____          Factors of 4: ____, ____

____ × ____ × ____ × ____ = ____

b) **15 × 8**          Factors of 15: ____, ____          Factors of 8: ____, ____

____ × ____ × ____ × ____ = ____

c) **35 × 6**          Factors of 35: ____, ____          Factors of 6: ____, ____

____ × ____ × ____ × ____ = ____

d) **45 × 4**          Factors of 45: ____, ____          Factors of 4: ____, ____

____ × ____ × ____ × ____ = ____

# Division

## Learn and revise

Break numbers up to help you work out division answers.

**Example:** What is 54 divided by 3?

Break 54 up into 30 and 24.

$$30 \div 3 = 10$$
$$24 \div 3 = 8$$
$$\text{So } 54 \div 3 = 18$$

Remember – if there are remainders in division problems, check that the answer makes sense. Should you round the answer up or down?

**Example:** 15 pencils are shared equally between four people. How many will each person get?

Three pencils each and three left over.

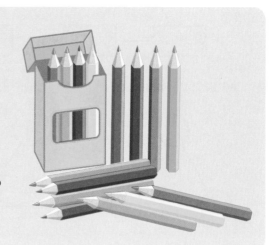

**Example:** A box can hold four pencils. How many boxes are needed for 15 pencils?

Four boxes, with one box of three pencils.

## Practice activities

1.  Answer these.

    a)  $60 \div 4 =$ _____

    b)  $85 \div 5 =$ _____

    c)  $57 \div 3 =$ _____

    d)  $72 \div 6 =$ _____

    e)  $91 \div 7 =$ _____

    f)  $92 \div 4 =$ _____

    g)  $78 \div 6 =$ _____

    h)  $84 \div 3 =$ _____

**2.** Divide these and join each division to the matching remainder.

61 ÷ 3

| no remainder |
|:---:|
| 1 |
| 2 |
| 3 |
| 4 |
| 5 |

84 ÷ 4

74 ÷ 6

92 ÷ 8

78 ÷ 5

86 ÷ 9

**3.** Complete each chart with the numbers coming out of each division machine.

**a)** IN → ÷3 → OUT

| IN | 900 | 1500 | 2100 | 1200 | 2400 | 2700 |
|:---:|:---:|:---:|:---:|:---:|:---:|:---:|
| OUT | 300 | | | | | |

**b)** IN → ÷4 → OUT

| IN | 800 | 2400 | 1200 | 3200 | 1600 | 2800 |
|:---:|:---:|:---:|:---:|:---:|:---:|:---:|
| OUT | 200 | | | | | |

**4.** Mr Wilson sells all types of tyres. Read and answer these questions.

**a)** There are 49 bicycle tyres. How many bicycles can have a set of tyres? _____

**b)** There are 73 car tyres. How many cars can have four new tyres? _____

**c)** Buses have six wheels and Mr Wilson has 85 bus tyres. How many buses can have a full set of new tyres?

_____

**d)** Mr Wilson stacks lorry tyres in piles of eight tyres.

How many full piles can he make with 45 tyres and how many tyres are left over?

_____ piles _____ tyres left over

# Mental arithmetic test 5

1. $8 \times 9 =$ _____

2. Answer both of these.

   $9 \times 4 \quad =$ _____

   $9 \times 400 =$ _____

3. $11 \times$ _____ $= 44$

4. $12 \times 7 =$ _____

5. $56 \div 7 =$ _____

6. What is the total weight of three cakes weighing 80 g each?

   _____ g

7. $90 \div 5 =$ _____

8. $40 \times 30 =$ _____

9. 40 balloons are needed for a party and there are 12 balloons in a pack.

   How many packs of balloons will be needed, and how many balloons will be left over?

   _____ packs

   _____ balloons left over

10. $3600 \div 4 =$ _____

11. Use factors to help multiply 14 by 6.

    Factors of 14: _____ _____

    Factors of 6: _____ _____

    _____ $\times$ _____ $\times$ _____ $\times$ _____ $=$ _____

12. $6 \times 700 =$ _____

13. Answer these.

    $6 \times 3 \quad =$ _____

    $6 \times 6 \quad =$ _____

    $6 \times 12 =$ _____

14. $4 \times 8 \times 2 =$ _____

15. $45 \div 6 =$ _____ r _____

16. What is 3500 divided by 5?

    _____

17. $50 \times 60 =$ _____

18. $8 \times 12 =$ _____

19. $84 \div 6 =$ _____

20. What is the remainder when 28 is divided by 3?

    r = _____

Score    /20

# Mental arithmetic test 6

1. 60 ÷ _____ = 5

2. 32 eggs are put into boxes each holding six eggs.

   How many full boxes will there be and how many eggs are left over?

   _____ full boxes

   _____ eggs left over

3. 81 ÷ 9 = _____

4. 8 × 7 = _____

5. Answer these.

   11 × 3  = _____

   11 × 6  = _____

   11 × 12 = _____

6. 48 ÷ 3 = _____

7. 1600 ÷ 2 = _____

8. 5 × 6 × 7 = _____

9. 51 ÷ 4 = _____ r _____

10. 12 × 9 = _____

11. What is the remainder when 38 is divided by 7?

    r = _____

12. 6 × 11 = _____

13. Answer both of these.

    6 × 9    = _____

    6 × 900 = _____

14. 56 ÷ 4 = _____

15. 70 × 40 = _____

16. Use factors to help multiply 35 by 4.

    Factors of 35: _____ _____

    Factors of 4: _____ _____

    _____ × _____ × _____ × _____ = _____

17. 700 × 7 = _____

18. 1800 ÷ 3 = _____

19. 11 × 12 = _____

20. 20 × 90 = _____

Score        /20

27

# Fractions

## Learn and revise

Remember that a fraction has two parts.

The **denominator** tells you the number of equal parts the whole is divided into. $\frac{2}{3}$ The **numerator** tells you the number of those equal parts that are taken.

This fraction strip shows some equivalent fractions.

Use the strip to show that $\frac{2}{3} = \frac{4}{6}$.

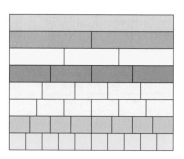

You can multiply or divide the denominator and numerator by the same number to make equivalent fractions.

## Practice activities

1. Write the pairs of equivalent fractions for each part shaded blue.

   a)
   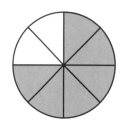

   ____ = ____

   b)
   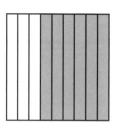
   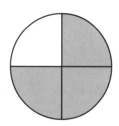

   ____ = ____

   c)
   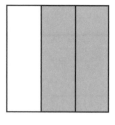

   ____ = ____

   d)

   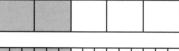

   ____ = ____

**2.** This circle is divided into tenths. Write the fraction for each colour.

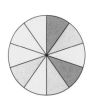

Red = $\dfrac{\Box}{10}$      Yellow = $\dfrac{\Box}{10}$      Green = $\dfrac{\Box}{10}$

Now write the fractions in order starting with the largest.

$\dfrac{\Box}{10}$ > $\dfrac{\Box}{10}$ > $\dfrac{\Box}{10}$

**3.** This rectangle is divided into 15 parts. Write a fraction for each colour.

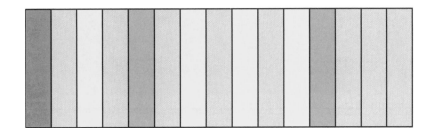

Red = $\dfrac{\Box}{15}$      Yellow = $\dfrac{\Box}{15}$      Green = $\dfrac{\Box}{15}$      Blue = $\dfrac{\Box}{15}$

Now write the fractions in order starting with the smallest.

$\dfrac{\Box}{15}$ < $\dfrac{\Box}{15}$ < $\dfrac{\Box}{15}$ < $\dfrac{\Box}{15}$

**4.** Complete the next equivalent fraction in each of these.

**a)** $\dfrac{3}{5} = \dfrac{6}{\Box} = \dfrac{\Box}{15} = \dfrac{12}{\Box} = \dfrac{\Box}{\Box} = \dfrac{\Box}{\Box}$

**b)** $\dfrac{3}{4} = \dfrac{\Box}{8} = \dfrac{9}{\Box} = \dfrac{\Box}{16} = \dfrac{\Box}{\Box} = \dfrac{\Box}{\Box}$

**c)** $\dfrac{7}{10} = \dfrac{14}{\Box} = \dfrac{\Box}{30} = \dfrac{28}{\Box} = \dfrac{\Box}{\Box} = \dfrac{\Box}{\Box}$

**d)** $\dfrac{3}{8} = \dfrac{\Box}{16} = \dfrac{9}{\Box} = \dfrac{\Box}{32} = \dfrac{\Box}{\Box} = \dfrac{\Box}{\Box}$

# Fractions of amounts

When you need to find fractions of amounts, use the numerator and denominator.

**Example:** What is $\frac{1}{5}$ of 20?

When the numerator is 1, just divide by the denominator.

$$\frac{1}{5} \text{ of } 20 = 20 \div 5 = 4$$

**Example:** What is $\frac{3}{5}$ of 20?

When the numerator is more than 1, divide by the denominator then multiply by the numerator.

$$\frac{1}{5} \text{ of } 20 = 4$$

$\frac{3}{5}$ is the same as $\frac{1}{5} \times 3$

$$\left(\frac{1}{5} + \frac{1}{5} + \frac{1}{5}\right)$$

So $\frac{3}{5}$ of $20 = 4 \times 3 = 12$

## Practice activities

1. Colour $\frac{3}{4}$ of each group of trees. Write each answer.

a) $\frac{3}{4}$ of 24 = _____

b) $\frac{3}{4}$ of 28 = _____

c) $\frac{3}{4}$ of 12 = _____

d) $\frac{3}{4}$ of 16 = _____

# Answers

**Pages 4–5**
1. a) 24, 36, 48    b) 50, 75, 175
   c) 36, 63, 72    d) 28, 35, 42
   e) 4000, 5000, 6000
2. a) 81, 76    b) 86, 89    c) 53, 47
   d) 480, 530    e) 159, 157
3. −11, −6, −1, 3, 12
   −15, −9, −7, −2, 8
4. a) 600    b) 953    c) 452    d) 689
5. a) 982, 992, 1002    b) 4010, 4020, 4030
   c) 959, 1059, 1159    d) 7023, 7123, 7223
   e) 1519, 2519, 3519    f) 7795, 8795, 9795

**Pages 6–7**
1. a) 10, 2    b) 1000, 400
   c) 700, 3    d) 6000, 800, 40
   e) 8000, 40, 7
2. a) 4532    b) 1026    c) 6703    d) 7599
3. a) 6528    b) 1985    c) 5731
4. a) 3345    b) 6756    c) 5251    d) 5003
5. a) 2305    b) 1743    c) 2168
6. a) – b) Check each number and word matches the beads
   drawn on each abacus.

**Pages 8–9**
1. a) <    b) >
   c) >    d) <
2. 1479, (1974)
3. a) 2087, 2900, 3149, 3150
   b) 5904, 5933, 6102, 6244
   c) 8003, 8030, 8300, 8303
   d) 8599, 8959, 9132, 9213
4. Everest – 8848 m; K2 – 8611 m; Lenin Peak – 7134 m;
   Aconcagua – 6960 m; McKinley – 6194 m;
   Kilimanjaro – 5893 m; Cook – 3766 m;
   Chappal Waddi – 2409 m

**Page 10**
1. −3, 7    2. 700, 30
3. 300, 250    4. 1476
5. 167, 162    6. 1596, 1956, 1965
7. 2371    8. 410
9. 3440, 3450    10. 5476, (7456)
11. 230    12. 32, 44
13. 982, 1082    14. 8915
15. 8351    16. 6701
17. −8, −5    18. 100, 104
19. >, <    20. 4470

**Page 11**
1. 2004, 2104    2. 2456
3. 205    4. 230, 250
5. 1422    6. <, >
7. 7887, 8787, 8877    8. 3604
9. −9, 2    10. 32, 56
11. 31, 34    12. −8, −4
13. 9000, 10    14. 1320
15. 3092, (3910)    16. 1790, 2790
17. 432, 232    18. 687
19. 4728    20. 1200

**Pages 12–13**
1.

| +  | 1  | 2  | 3  | 4  | 5  | 6  | 7  | 8  | 9  | 10 |
|----|----|----|----|----|----|----|----|----|----|----|
| 1  | 2  | 3  | 4  | 5  | 6  | 7  | 8  | 9  | 10 | 11 |
| 2  | 3  | 4  | 5  | 6  | 7  | 8  | 9  | 10 | 11 | 12 |
| 3  | 4  | 5  | 6  | 7  | 8  | 9  | 10 | 11 | 12 | 13 |
| 4  | 5  | 6  | 7  | 8  | 9  | 10 | 11 | 12 | 13 | 14 |
| 5  | 6  | 7  | 8  | 9  | 10 | 11 | 12 | 13 | 14 | 15 |
| 6  | 7  | 8  | 9  | 10 | 11 | 12 | 13 | 14 | 15 | 16 |
| 7  | 8  | 9  | 10 | 11 | 12 | 13 | 14 | 15 | 16 | 17 |
| 8  | 9  | 10 | 11 | 12 | 13 | 14 | 15 | 16 | 17 | 18 |
| 9  | 10 | 11 | 12 | 13 | 14 | 15 | 16 | 17 | 18 | 19 |
| 10 | 11 | 12 | 13 | 14 | 15 | 16 | 17 | 18 | 19 | 20 |

2. a) 15    b) 5    c) 4
   d) 15    e) 7    f) 6
3. a) 140    b) 110
   c) 50    d) 110, 50, 60
   e) 130, 50, 80    f) 80, 50, 30

**Pages 14–15**
1. a) 82    b) 67
   c) 43    d) 93
   e) 71    f) 72
   g) 71    h) 87
2. a) 131    b) 114
   c) 115    d) 108
   e) 424    f) 317
   g) 261    h) 319
3. a)

| +   | 80  | 60  | 90  | 70  |
|-----|-----|-----|-----|-----|
| 253 | 333 | 313 | 343 | 323 |
| 185 | 265 | 245 | 275 | 255 |
| 693 | 773 | 753 | 783 | 763 |

b)

| +  | 45 | 38 | 52 | 27 |
|----|----|----|----|----|
| 35 | 80 | 73 | 87 | 62 |
| 26 | 71 | 64 | 78 | 53 |
| 41 | 86 | 79 | 93 | 68 |

4. 45 + **3**8 = 8**3**, **5**6 + 14 = **7**0, 19 + 4**4** = **6**3, **1**7 + 35 = 5**2**
5. 60

**Pages 16–17**
1. a) 37    b) 16
   c) 39    d) 47
   e) 29    f) 18
2. a) 95    b) 78
   c) 72    d) 71
   e) 78
3. a) Bottom row should be completed as follows:
      93, 35, 62, 41, 79
   b) Bottom row should be completed as follows:
      650, 150, 450, 550, 350

# Answers

**4.** **a)** 45 cm  **b)** 35 cm
  **c)** 55 cm  **d)** 20 cm
  **e)** 30 cm

## Page 18
| | | | |
|---|---|---|---|
| **1.** | 80 | **2.** | 61 |
| **3.** | 80 | **4.** | 521 |
| **5.** | 618 | **6.** | 80 |
| **7.** | 155 | **8.** | 56 |
| **9.** | 250, 550 | **10.** | 33 |
| **11.** | 53 | **12.** | 8 |
| **13.** | 86 | **14.** | 49 |
| **15.** | 521, 237 | **16.** | 126 |
| **17.** | 81 | **18.** | 57 |
| **19.** | 99 | **20.** | 62 |

## Page 19
| | | | |
|---|---|---|---|
| **1.** | 75 | **2.** | 94 kg |
| **3.** | 64 | **4.** | 311 |
| **5.** | 285 | **6.** | 8 |
| **7.** | 280 | **8.** | 35 |
| **9.** | 114 | **10.** | 90 |
| **11.** | 210, 166 | **12.** | 425 |
| **13.** | 84 | **14.** | 350 ml |
| **15.** | 130 | **16.** | 552 |
| **17.** | 467, 276 | **18.** | 203 |
| **19.** | 26 | **20.** | 37 |

## Pages 20–21
**1.** **a)** $7 \times 5 = 35, 5 \times 7 = 35, 35 \div 5 = 7, 35 \div 7 = 5$
  **b)** $6 \times 7 = 42, 7 \times 6 = 42, 42 \div 6 = 7, 42 \div 7 = 6$
  **c)** $9 \times 4 = 36, 4 \times 9 = 36, 36 \div 9 = 4, 36 \div 4 = 9$
  **d)** $8 \times 6 = 48, 6 \times 8 = 48, 48 \div 6 = 8, 48 \div 8 = 6$
  **e)** $11 \times 12 = 132, 12 \times 11 = 132, 132 \div 11 = 12, 132 \div 12 = 11$

**2.** **a)** 54    **b)** 9
  **c)** 6    **d)** 9
  **e)** 7    **f)** 77

**3.** **a)** 36    **b)** 15, 30, 60
  **c)** 24, 48, 96   **d)** 12, 24, 48
  **e)** 27, 54, 108  **f)** 21, 42, 84

**4.** 88, 28, 27, 42
  72, 22, 36, 80
  21, 18, 18, 121
  60, 56, 81, 48

**5.** **a)** 56   **b)** 7   **c)** 21   **d)** 9

## Pages 22–23
**1.** **a)** 36, 3600  **b)** 48, 4800
  **c)** 56, 5600  **d)** 27, 2700
  **e)** 49, 4900  **f)** 48, 4800

**2.**

| × | 30 | 60 | 80 |
|---|---|---|---|
| **20** | 600 | 1200 | 1600 |
| **90** | 2700 | 5400 | 7200 |
| **40** | 1200 | 2400 | 3200 |

**3.** **a)** 600   **b)** 9
  **c)** 2400   **d)** 500
  **e)** 2800   **f)** 300

**4.** **a)** 60   **b)** 240
  **c)** 120   **d)** 90

**5.** **a)** Factors of 25: 5, 5
    Factors of 4: 2, 2    $5 \times 5 \times 2 \times 2 = 100$
  **b)** Factors of 15: 3, 5
    Factors of 8: 2, 4    $3 \times 5 \times 2 \times 4 = 120$
  **c)** Factors of 35: 5, 7
    Factors of 6: 2, 3    $5 \times 7 \times 2 \times 3 = 210$
  **d)** Factors of 45: 5, 9
    Factors of 4: 2, 2    $5 \times 9 \times 2 \times 2 = 180$

## Pages 24–25
**1.** **a)** 15   **b)** 17   **c)** 19
  **d)** 12   **e)** 13   **f)** 23
  **g)** 13   **h)** 28

**2.** no remainder $\rightarrow 84 \div 4$
  $1 \rightarrow 61 \div 3$
  $2 \rightarrow 74 \div 6$
  $3 \rightarrow 78 \div 5$
  $4 \rightarrow 92 \div 8$
  $5 \rightarrow 86 \div 9$

**3.** **a)** Bottom row should be completed as follows:
    500, 700, 400, 800, 900
  **b)** Bottom row should be completed as follows:
    600, 300, 800, 400, 700

**4.** **a)** 24    **b)** 18
  **c)** 14    **d)** 5 piles, 5 tyres left over

## Page 26
| | | | |
|---|---|---|---|
| **1.** | 72 | **2.** | 36, 3600 |
| **3.** | 4 | **4.** | 84 |
| **5.** | 8 | **6.** | 240 g |
| **7.** | 18 | **8.** | 1200 |
| **9.** | 4 packs, 8 balloons left over | **10.** | 900 |

**11.** Factors of 14: 2, 7   Factors of 6: 2, 3
  $2 \times 7 \times 2 \times 3 = 84$

| | | | |
|---|---|---|---|
| **12.** | 4200 | **13.** | 18, 36, 72 |
| **14.** | 64 | **15.** | 7 r 3 |
| **16.** | 700 | **17.** | 3000 |
| **18.** | 96 | **19.** | 14 |
| **20.** | r = 1 | | |

## Page 27
| | | | |
|---|---|---|---|
| **1.** | 12 | **2.** | 5 full boxes and 2 eggs left over |
| **3.** | 9 | **4.** | 56 |
| **5.** | 33, 66, 132 | **6.** | 16 |
| **7.** | 800 | **8.** | 210 |
| **9.** | 12 r 3 | **10.** | 108 |
| **11.** | r = 3 | **12.** | 66 |
| **13.** | 54, 5400 | **14.** | 14 |
| **15.** | 2800 | | |

**16.** Factors of 35: 5, 7   Factors of 4: 2, 2
  $5 \times 7 \times 2 \times 2 = 140$

| | | | |
|---|---|---|---|
| **17.** | 4900 | **18.** | 600 |
| **19.** | 132 | **20.** | 1800 |

## Pages 28–29
**1.** **a)** $\frac{3}{4}, \frac{6}{8}$    **b)** $\frac{2}{3}, \frac{6}{9}$
  **c)** $\frac{4}{5}, \frac{8}{10}$    **d)** $\frac{2}{5}, \frac{6}{15}$

**2.** Red = $\frac{2}{10}$    Yellow = $\frac{5}{10}$    Green = $\frac{3}{10}$
  $\frac{5}{10} > \frac{3}{10} > \frac{2}{10}$

**3.** Red = $\frac{1}{15}$    Yellow = $\frac{4}{15}$    Green = $\frac{8}{15}$    Blue = $\frac{2}{15}$
  $\frac{1}{15} < \frac{2}{15} < \frac{4}{15} < \frac{8}{15}$

**4.** **a)** $\frac{6}{10}, \frac{9}{15}, \frac{12}{20}, \frac{15}{25}, \frac{18}{30}$
  **b)** $\frac{6}{8}, \frac{9}{12}, \frac{12}{16}, \frac{15}{20}, \frac{18}{24}$
  **c)** $\frac{14}{20}, \frac{21}{30}, \frac{28}{40}, \frac{35}{50}, \frac{42}{60}$
  **d)** $\frac{6}{16}, \frac{9}{24}, \frac{12}{32}, \frac{15}{40}, \frac{18}{48}$

## Pages 30–31
**1.** **a)** 18   **b)** 21
  **c)** 9   **d)** 12

**2.** **a)** 11, 22   **b)** 12, 36
  **c)** 7, 28   **d)** 6, 30
  **e)** 8, 56   **f)** 3, 15

**3.** $\frac{3}{5}$ of 40 = 24, $\frac{3}{4}$ of 40 = 30, $\frac{5}{8}$ of 40 = 25, so $\frac{3}{4}$ of 40

**4.** **a)** >   **b)** >
  **c)** <   **d)** >
  **e)** <   **f)** <

**5.** silver $\rightarrow$ 24
  red $\rightarrow$ 18
  white $\rightarrow$ 10
  black $\rightarrow$ 8

**Pages 32–33**

1. a) $\frac{4}{100}$, 0.04      b) $\frac{9}{100}$, 0.09
   c) $\frac{15}{100}$, 0.15      d) $\frac{2}{10}$, 0.2
   e) $\frac{22}{100}$, 0.22      f) $\frac{28}{100}$, 0.28

2. a) $\frac{2}{4}$ or $\frac{1}{2}$      b) $\frac{4}{6}$ or $\frac{2}{3}$
   c) $\frac{8}{10}$ or $\frac{4}{5}$      d) $\frac{4}{8}$ or $\frac{1}{2}$ (or $\frac{2}{4}$)

3. a) $\frac{2}{8}$ (or $\frac{1}{4}$)      b) $\frac{2}{10}$ (or $\frac{1}{5}$)
   c) $\frac{3}{5}$      d) $\frac{6}{10}$ (or $\frac{3}{5}$)

4. 

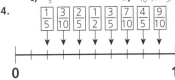

**Page 34**

1. Any 8 parts shaded; any 4 parts shaded
2. <      3. $\frac{9}{10}$, $\frac{2}{10}$
4. 2      5. $\frac{2}{3}$, $\frac{4}{6}$
6. $\frac{16}{20}$      7. $\frac{4}{8}$ (or $\frac{1}{2}$ or $\frac{2}{4}$)
8. 

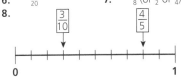

9. $\frac{10}{12}$, $\frac{15}{18}$      10. $\frac{4}{10} < \frac{6}{10} < \frac{8}{10}$
11. $\frac{13}{100}$      12. $\frac{5}{10}$ or $\frac{1}{2}$
13. Any 5 parts blue; any 2 parts red
14. 5, 15
15. 10 pink, 8 blue and 42 white
16. $\frac{9}{18}$      17. $\frac{4}{5}$
18. $\frac{4}{5}$ of 40      19. $\frac{5}{10}$ (or $\frac{1}{2}$)
20. 0.39

**Page 35**

1. 4, 20      2. $\frac{5}{7}$
3. $\frac{8}{10}$, $\frac{4}{10}$
4. Any 6 parts shaded; any 9 parts shaded
5. $\frac{4}{16}$      6. 18
7. $\frac{3}{4}$, $\frac{15}{20}$      8. >
9. $\frac{4}{7}$      10. 0.17
11. $\frac{4}{5}$
12. 

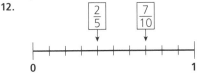

13. Any 7 parts blue; any 4 parts red
14. $\frac{12}{20}$      15. $\frac{6}{14}$, $\frac{9}{21}$
16. $\frac{5}{6}$ of 30      17. $\frac{5}{10}$ (or $\frac{1}{2}$)
18. $\frac{28}{100}$      19. $\frac{2}{10} < \frac{3}{10} < \frac{9}{10}$
20. 15 cows, 10 goats, 25 sheep

**Pages 36–37**

1. a) 8      b) 91
   c) 356      d) 4.2
   e) 0.7      f) 83.5
2. a) 194      b) 520
   c) 3495      d) 60
   e) 2      f) 4705
3. a) 9.6      b) 0.8
   c) 14.3      d) 0.52
   e) 0.04      f) 0.706
4. a) 6.74      b) 28.9
   c) 0.71      d) 0.352
   e) 0.109      f) 0.4

5. a) ×10      b) ÷100
   c) ×100      d) ÷100
   e) ×10      f) ÷100

**Pages 38–39**

1. a) 3.5, 5.3, 5.6, 6.3, 6.5
   b) 11.6, 11.8, 12.1, 12.3, 12.5
   c) 22.7, 22.9, 23.1, 23.6, 23.8
2. a) 0.25, 0.55, 0.81, 0.85, 0.92
   b) 2.95, 3.17, 3.22, 3.25, 3.27
   c) 8.51, 8.54, 9.06, 9.09, 9.56
3. Gold medal – 7.13 m; Silver medal – 7.05 m; Bronze medal – 7.04 m; 4th place – 6.91 m; 5th place – 6.85 m; 6th place – 6.83 m
4. a) 3      b) 4
   c) 4      d) 5
   e) 6      f) 6
5. a) 1      b) 8
   c) 3      d) 20
   e) 35      f) 26

**Pages 40–41**

1. a) 1.1      b) 1.3
   c) 1.4      d) 1.4
   e) 1.4      f) 1.5
2. a) 1.4      b) 0.7
   c) 1.4      d) 0.5
   e) 0.8      f) 0.8
3. 0.8 + 0.4 → 1.2
   1.6 – 1.2 → 0.4
   1.3 – 0.5 → 0.8
   0.6 + 0.8 → 1.4
   1.5 – 0.9 → 0.6
   1.7 – 1.5 → 0.2
   0.9 + 0.9 → 1.8
   1.2 + 0.4 → 1.6
4. 0.8 + 0.7 = 1.**5**
   1.**4** – 0.7 = 0.7
   **0.4** + 0.9 = 1.3
   **1.2** – 0.8 = 0.4

**Page 42**

1. 4.6 < 6.4 < 6.7 < 7.4 < 7.6      2. 19
3. 0.54      4. 1.25
5. ×100, ×10      6. 14, 1.4
7. 0.318      8. 5, 11
9. 4      10. 1.3, 0.7
11. 6710      12. 13.2
13. 1.1      14. 1.38 < 1.83 < 3.18 < 8.13 < 8.31
15. 0.45      16. 1.6
17. 10, 12      18. ÷, ×
19. 50.7      20. ÷10, ÷100

**Page 43**

1. 11, 1.1      2. 7, 15
3. 2      4. 2.5 < 2.7 < 5.2 < 7.2 < 7.5
5. 1.7, 0.8      6. 5.7
7. ×10, ×100      8. 0.04
9. 0.5      10. 5, 0.5
11. 1475      12. 0.219
13. ÷100, ÷10      14. 1.4
15. 5, 12      16. 0.8
17. 609      18. 10.1 < 10.9 < 90.1 < 90.9 < 99.1
19. 0.06      20. ×, ÷

**Pages 44–45**

1. a) 0.55 m      b) 3500 g
   c) 3500 ml      d) 128 cm
   e) 4 l 200 ml      f) 2 kg 450 g
   g) 8000 m      h) 7 cm 5 mm
   i) 3.2 m      j) 2 km

# Answers

**2.** a) >  b) =
    c) >  d) <
    e) =  f) <
    g) >  h) >
**3.** a) 5  b) 3
    c) 6  d) 17
    e) 64  f) 5
**4.** 4

**Pages 46–47**
**1.** a) £1.84  b) £2.52
    c) £1.80  d) £2.37
**2.** a) £4.60  b) £1.70
    c) £3.90  d) £4.80
    e) £1.10  f) £1.50
**3.** a) 20p  b) 70p
    c) 5p  d) 25p
    e) £1.10  f) 95p
**4.**

Ice-lollies

|  |  | 0 | 1 | 2 | 3 | 4 |
|---|---|---|---|---|---|---|
| Ice-creams | **0** | 0 | 20p | 40p | 60p | **80p** |
| | **1** | 50p | 70p | **90p** | **£1.10** | **£1.30** |
| | **2** | £1.00 | £1.20 | **£1.40** | **£1.60** | **£1.80** |
| | **3** | £1.50 | **£1.70** | **£1.90** | **£2.10** | **£2.30** |
| | **4** | **£2.00** | **£2.20** | **£2.40** | **£2.60** | **£2.80** |

3 ice-creams; 4 ice-lollies

**Pages 48–49**
**1.** a) 2:45  b) 10:05
    c) 6:40  d) 8:33
    e) 1:17  f) 9:59
    g) 11:03  h) 6:21
**2. a)**  afternoon  **b)**  morning  **c)** morning

**d)**  evening  **e)** afternoon  **f)**  evening

**3.** a) 9.15 a.m.  b) 11.30 a.m.
    c) 4.35 p.m.  d) 8.55 p.m.
    e) 12.25 p.m.  f) 12.35 p.m.
**4.** a) 5 minutes  b) 28 days
    c) 150 seconds  d) 270 minutes
    e) 42 months  f) 8 weeks
    g) 10 days  h) 2 hours
    i) 1800 seconds  j) 168 hours

**Page 50**
**1.** 4 kg 810 g  **2.** 850 mm
**3.** 5 kg  **4.** 1600 ml
**5.** 9.26 a.m., 3.55 p.m.  **6.** 7000 m
**7.** 30p  **8.** 180 minutes
**9.** 1530 cm  **10.** <, =
**11.** £2.90  **12.** 3 m
**13.** 3.45 p.m.  **14.** 7500 g
**15.** morning  **16.** £4.25
**17.** 24 l, 1 km  **18.** 48 hours
**19.** 11.46 a.m.  **20.** £1.75

**Page 51**
**1.** 10 kg, 13 m  **2.** £2.70
**3.** 4200 ml  **4.** 8.5 m
**5.** 5.45 p.m.  **6.** £3.35
**7.** 1300 g  **8.** >, <
**9.** evening  **10.** 2 km
**11.** 4 l 700 ml  **12.** £3.80
**13.** 10.18 a.m., 4.32 p.m.  **14.** 36 months
**15.** 12 km  **16.** 10 minutes
**17.** 1.2 km  **18.** 50p
**19.** 21 days  **20.** 8 kg 250 g

**Page 52**
**1.** 5  **2.** 17  **3.** 19  **4.** 14
**5.** 120  **6.** 40  **7.** 15  **8.** 21
**9.** 13  **10.** 70  **11.** 9  **12.** 100
**13.** 9  **14.** 90  **15.** 21  **16.** 48
**17.** 14  **18.** 50  **19.** 9  **20.** 14
**21.** 20  **22.** 80  **23.** 8  **24.** 3
**25.** 13  **26.** 8  **27.** 12  **28.** 8
**29.** 6  **30.** 6  **31.** 14  **32.** 11
**33.** 6  **34.** 15  **35.** 5  **36.** 13
**37.** 12  **38.** 8  **39.** 11  **40.** 7

**Page 54**
**1.** 42  **2.** 36  **3.** 28  **4.** 4
**5.** 88  **6.** 30  **7.** 27  **8.** 7
**9.** 10  **10.** 60  **11.** 99  **12.** 64
**13.** 11  **14.** 3  **15.** 21  **16.** 25
**17.** 72  **18.** 9  **19.** 7  **20.** 15
**21.** 6  **22.** 54  **23.** 6  **24.** 5
**25.** 9  **26.** 12  **27.** 36  **28.** 9
**29.** 6  **30.** 7  **31.** 40  **32.** 0
**33.** 14  **34.** 6  **35.** 84  **36.** 48
**37.** 3  **38.** 8  **39.** 56  **40.** 2

**Page 56**
**1.** 36  **2.** 14  **3.** 11  **4.** 5
**5.** 8  **6.** 130  **7.** 30  **8.** 70
**9.** 56  **10.** 60  **11.** 6  **12.** 120
**13.** 10  **14.** 180  **15.** 22  **16.** 33
**17.** 36  **18.** 7  **19.** 6  **20.** 3
**21.** 110  **22.** 90  **23.** 7  **24.** 4
**25.** 15  **26.** 64  **27.** 17  **28.** 5
**29.** 8  **30.** 5  **31.** 11  **32.** 40
**33.** 120  **34.** 9  **35.** 7  **36.** 20
**37.** 5  **38.** 54  **39.** 36  **40.** 16

**2.** Answer each pair of questions.

    **a)** $\frac{1}{3}$ of 33 = _____      **b)** $\frac{1}{4}$ of 48 = _____      **c)** $\frac{1}{5}$ of 35 = _____

       $\frac{2}{3}$ of 33 = _____         $\frac{3}{4}$ of 48 = _____         $\frac{4}{5}$ of 35 = _____

    **d)** $\frac{1}{6}$ of 36 = _____      **e)** $\frac{1}{10}$ of 80 = _____      **f)** $\frac{1}{8}$ of 24 = _____

       $\frac{5}{6}$ of 36 = _____         $\frac{7}{10}$ of 80 = _____       $\frac{5}{8}$ of 24 = _____

**3.** Here are 40 flowers.

Which would give you the greatest number of flowers, $\frac{3}{5}$, $\frac{3}{4}$ or $\frac{5}{8}$ of them? Tick the correct answer.

$\frac{3}{5}$ of 40 = _____

$\frac{3}{4}$ of 40 = _____

$\frac{5}{8}$ of 40 = _____

**4.** Complete by writing < or > between each pair of amounts.

    **a)** $\frac{1}{3}$ of 30 ☐ $\frac{1}{5}$ of 30

    **b)** $\frac{1}{4}$ of 20 ☐ $\frac{1}{5}$ of 20

    **c)** $\frac{1}{10}$ of 50 ☐ $\frac{1}{5}$ of 50

    **d)** $\frac{1}{8}$ of 40 ☐ $\frac{1}{10}$ of 40

    **e)** $\frac{1}{10}$ of 60 ☐ $\frac{1}{3}$ of 60

    **f)** $\frac{1}{5}$ of 100 ☐ $\frac{1}{4}$ of 100

**5.** In a car park there are 60 cars. How many of each colour are there in total?

    $\frac{2}{5}$ are silver = _____        $\frac{1}{6}$ are white = _____

    $\frac{3}{10}$ are red = _____        $\frac{2}{15}$ are black = _____

# Fraction problems

This number line is divided into tenths and hundredths. They are written as common fractions (e.g. $\frac{1}{100}$) and as decimal fractions (e.g. 0.01).

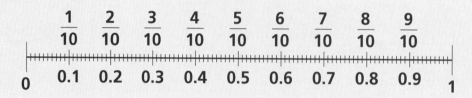

If we zoom into the numbers between 0 and $\frac{1}{10}$, we can count in hundredths.

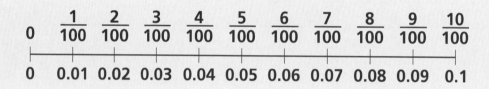

$\frac{1}{100}$ = 0.01    zero point zero one

$\frac{2}{100}$ = 0.02    zero point zero two

## Practice activities

1.  Write both the common fraction and decimal fraction for each arrow.

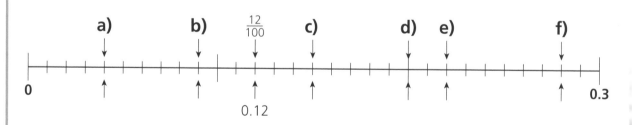

a) \_\_\_ \_\_\_                    b) \_\_\_ \_\_\_

c) \_\_\_ \_\_\_                    d) \_\_\_ \_\_\_

e) \_\_\_ \_\_\_                    f) \_\_\_ \_\_\_

*It is easy to add and subtract fractions with the same denominator – just add or subtract the numerators.*

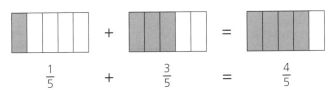

$$\frac{1}{5} \quad + \quad \frac{3}{5} \quad = \quad \frac{4}{5}$$

**2.** Add these fractions.

**a)**  $\frac{1}{4} + \frac{1}{4}$ = _____ or _____

**b)** 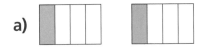 $\frac{2}{6} + \frac{2}{6}$ = _____ or _____

**c)** 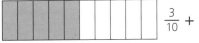 $\frac{3}{10} + \frac{5}{10}$ = _____ or _____

**d)**  $\frac{1}{8} + \frac{3}{8}$ = _____ or _____

**3.** Subtract these fractions.

**a)** $\frac{5}{8} - \frac{3}{8}$ = _____          **b)** $\frac{3}{10} - \frac{1}{10}$ = _____

**c)** $\frac{4}{5} - \frac{1}{5}$ = _____          **d)** $\frac{9}{10} - \frac{3}{10}$ = _____

**4.** Write each of these fractions in the correct position on the number line.

$$\frac{2}{5} \qquad \frac{1}{2} \qquad \frac{7}{10} \qquad \frac{3}{10} \qquad \frac{3}{5} \qquad \frac{9}{10} \qquad \frac{1}{5} \qquad \frac{4}{5}$$

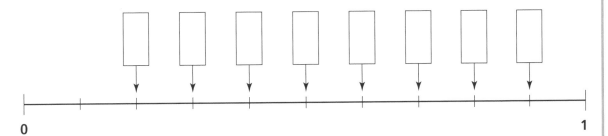

0                                                    1

# Mental arithmetic test 7

**1.** Colour $\frac{2}{3}$ of each rectangle.

**2.** Write < or > to make this true.

$\frac{1}{10}$ of 20 _____ $\frac{1}{5}$ of 20

**3.** Circle the largest fraction and underline the smallest fraction.

$\frac{7}{10}$    $\frac{2}{10}$    $\frac{9}{10}$    $\frac{5}{10}$    $\frac{3}{10}$

**4.** A box has 12 eggs. $\frac{1}{6}$ of the eggs are broken. How many eggs are broken?

_____

**5.** Write the pair of equivalent fractions for each part shaded blue.

_____      _____

**6.** Write the next equivalent fraction.

$\frac{4}{5} = \frac{8}{10} = \frac{12}{15} = \frac{\square}{\square}$

**7.** $\frac{7}{8} - \frac{3}{8} =$ _____

**8.** Write $\frac{3}{10}$ and $\frac{4}{5}$ in the correct positions on this number line.

**9.** Write the missing numbers in this equivalent fractions chain.

$\frac{5}{6} = \frac{\square}{12} = \frac{15}{\square}$

**10.** Write these in order, smallest first.

$\frac{4}{10}$      $\frac{8}{10}$      $\frac{6}{10}$

_____ < _____ < _____

**11.** This arrow is at 0.13. Circle the matching common fraction.

$\frac{3}{10}$     $\frac{1}{3}$     $\frac{13}{100}$     $\frac{30}{100}$

**12.** $\frac{4}{10} + \frac{1}{10} =$ _____ or _____

**13.** Shade $\frac{5}{8}$ of this rectangle blue and $\frac{1}{4}$ of the rectangle red.

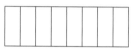

**14.** Answer these.

$\frac{1}{8}$ of 40 = _____     $\frac{3}{8}$ of 40 = _____

**15.** There are 60 flowers in a vase. Write how many of each colour.

$\frac{1}{6}$ pink  = _____

$\frac{2}{15}$ blue  = _____

$\frac{7}{10}$ white = _____

**16.** Circle the fraction that is equivalent to $\frac{3}{6}$.

$\frac{6}{9}$     $\frac{9}{18}$     $\frac{12}{18}$

**17.** $\frac{2}{5} + \frac{2}{5} =$ _____

**18.** Underline the greatest amount.

$\frac{3}{4}$ of 40     $\frac{7}{10}$ of 40     $\frac{4}{5}$ of 40

**19.** $\frac{9}{10} - \frac{4}{10} =$ _____

**20.** Circle the correct decimal fraction to match $\frac{39}{100}$.

0.39      3.9

0.039      3.09

Score    /20

34

**1.** Answer these.

$\frac{1}{6}$ of 24 = _____

$\frac{5}{6}$ of 24 = _____

**2.** $\frac{2}{7} + \frac{3}{7} =$ _____

**3.** Circle the largest fraction and underline the smallest fraction.

$\frac{4}{10}$     $\frac{8}{10}$     $\frac{5}{10}$     $\frac{6}{10}$     $\frac{7}{10}$

**4.** Colour $\frac{3}{5}$ of each rectangle.

**5.** Write the next equivalent fraction.

$\frac{1}{4} = \frac{2}{8} = \frac{3}{12} = \frac{\Box}{\Box}$

**6.** There are 30 children in a class and $\frac{3}{5}$ are girls.
How many girls are there? _____

**7.** Write the pair of equivalent fractions for each part shaded blue.

_____          _____

**8.** Write < or > to make this true.

$\frac{1}{3}$ of 60 _____ $\frac{1}{4}$ of 60

**9.** $\frac{6}{7} - \frac{2}{7} =$ _____

**10.** This arrow is at $\frac{17}{100}$. Circle the matching decimal fraction.

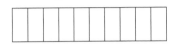

0             0.1            0.2

1.7     0.17     0.017     0.07

**11.** $\frac{1}{5} + \frac{3}{5} =$ _____

**12.** Write $\frac{7}{10}$ and $\frac{2}{5}$ in the correct positions on this number line.

0                                1

**13.** Shade $\frac{7}{12}$ of this rectangle blue and $\frac{1}{3}$ red.

**14.** Circle the fraction that is equivalent to $\frac{3}{5}$.

$\frac{6}{15}$         $\frac{15}{20}$         $\frac{12}{20}$

**15.** Write the missing numbers in this equivalent fractions chain.

$\frac{3}{7} = \frac{\Box}{14} = \frac{9}{\Box}$

**16.** Underline the greatest amount.

$\frac{3}{5}$ of 30        $\frac{2}{3}$ of 30        $\frac{5}{6}$ of 30

**17.** $\frac{8}{10} - \frac{3}{10} =$ _____

**18.** Circle the correct common fraction to match 0.28.

$\frac{2}{10}$     $\frac{2}{8}$     $\frac{20}{100}$     $\frac{28}{100}$

**19.** Write these in order, smallest first.

$\frac{9}{10}$        $\frac{3}{10}$        $\frac{2}{10}$

_____ < _____ < _____

**20.** A farmer has 50 animals. Write how many of each type.

$\frac{3}{10}$ cows = _____

$\frac{1}{5}$ goats = _____

$\frac{1}{2}$ sheep = _____

Score       /20

# Decimals

## Learn and revise

Follow these rules for multiplying and dividing numbers by 10 and 100.

| To multiply by 10 | To multiply by 100 |
|---|---|
| Move the digits **one** place to the **left**. 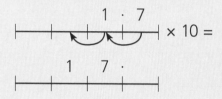 | Move the digits **two** places to the **left**. 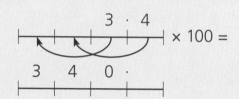 |

| To divide by 10 | To divide by 100 |
|---|---|
| Move the digits **one** place to the **right**. | Move the digits **two** places to the **right**. 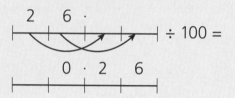 |

Fill any spaces with zeros. Putting a zero on the end of a decimal does not change the number.

1.2 is the same as 1.20 and 1.200

## Practice activities

1. Multiply these by 10 and write the answers.

   a) $0.8 \times 10 =$ _____

   b) $9.1 \times 10 =$ _____

   c) $35.6 \times 10 =$ _____

   d) $0.42 \times 10 =$ _____

   e) $0.07 \times 10 =$ _____

   f) $8.35 \times 10 =$ _____

**2.** Multiply these by 100 and write the answers.

    **a)**  1.94 × 100  = _____

    **b)**  5.2 × 100  = _____

    **c)**  34.95 × 100 = _____

    **d)**  0.6 × 100  = _____

    **e)**  0.02 × 100  = _____

    **f)**  47.05 × 100 = _____

**3.** Divide these by 10 and write the answers.

    **a)**  96 ÷ 10  = _____

    **b)**  8 ÷ 10  = _____

    **c)**  143 ÷ 10  = _____

    **d)**  5.2 ÷ 10  = _____

    **e)**  0.4 ÷ 10  = _____

    **f)**  7.06 ÷ 10  = _____

**4.** Divide these by 100 and write the answers.

    **a)**  674 ÷ 100  = _____

    **b)**  2890 ÷ 100 = _____

    **c)**  71 ÷ 100  = _____

    **d)**  35.2 ÷ 100 = _____

    **e)**  10.9 ÷ 100 = _____

    **f)**  40 ÷ 100  = _____

**5.** Write the missing operation on the blank bead in each of these. Is it **×10**, **×100**, **÷10** or **÷100**?

    **a)**  1.5 ⟶ ◯ ⟶ 15

    **b)**  29 ⟶ ◯ ⟶ 0.29

    **c)**  6.29 ⟶ ◯ ⟶ 629

    **d)**  580 ⟶ ◯ ⟶ 5.8

    **e)**  74.3 ⟶ ◯ ⟶ 743

    **f)**  8 ⟶ ◯ ⟶ 0.08

# Ordering and rounding decimals

## Learn and revise

When you compare and order tenths or hundredths, look carefully at the value of each digit.

**Example:** Put these in order, starting with the smallest:

3.4    3.8    2.9    4.3

Look at the whole numbers and then the tenths. The order is:

2.9    3.4    3.8    4.3

**Example:** Put these in order, starting with the smallest:

1.65    1.05    1.68    0.65

Look at the whole numbers, then the tenths, then the hundredths. The order is:

0.65    1.05    1.65    1.68

Decimal numbers can be rounded to the nearest whole number.

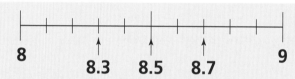

When rounding decimals look at the tenths digit:

- If it is 5 or more, round up to the next whole number.
- If it is less than 5, round down and the whole number stays the same.

8.<u>7</u> rounds up to 9

8.<u>3</u> rounds down to 8

8.<u>5</u> rounds up to 9

## Practice activities

1.  Write each set of numbers in order, starting with the smallest.

    a) | 5.6    6.3    5.3    6.5    3.5 |    ____  ____  ____  ____  ____
                                                    smallest

    b) | 11.8    12.5    11.6    12.1    12.3 |    ____  ____  ____  ____  ____
                                                        smallest

    c) | 23.6    23.1    22.9    23.8    22.7 |    ____  ____  ____  ____  ____
                                                        smallest

# Ordering and rounding decimals

**2.** Write each set of numbers in order, starting with the smallest.

**a)**

| 0.85 | 0.92 | 0.55 |
|------|------|------|
| 0.81 | 0.25 | |

____ ____ ____ ____ ____

smallest

**b)**

| 3.27 | 3.25 | 3.17 |
|------|------|------|
| 3.22 | 2.95 | |

____ ____ ____ ____ ____

smallest

**c)**

| 9.06 | 8.54 | 9.09 |
|------|------|------|
| 9.56 | 8.51 | |

____ ____ ____ ____ ____

smallest

**3.** These are the lengths in metres jumped by six long-jump athletes. Write the lengths in order starting with the longest.

| | |
|--|--|
| **Gold medal** | m |
| **Silver medal** | m |
| **Bronze medal** | m |
| **4th place** | m |
| **5th place** | m |
| **6th place** | m |

6.91  6.85  7.04  7.05  7.13  6.83

**4.** Round each decimal number to the nearest whole number. Use the number line to help you.

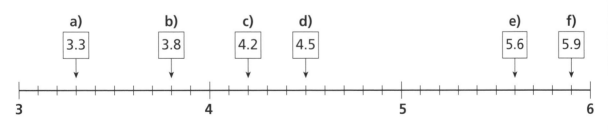

a) 3.3    b) 3.8    c) 4.2    d) 4.5    e) 5.6    f) 5.9

a) ____    b) ____    c) ____    d) ____    e) ____    f) ____

**5.** Round each of these to the nearest whole number.

**a)** 1.3 ⟶ ____    **b)** 7.8 ⟶ ____    **c)** 2.5 ⟶ ____

**d)** 20.1 ⟶ ____    **e)** 34.6 ⟶ ____    **f)** 25.7 ⟶ ____

# Decimal calculations

## Learn and revise

These both show that 0.8 + 0.5 = 1.3.

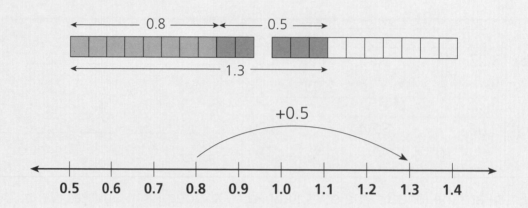

Use facts you know to calculate with decimals.

| | |
|---|---|
| 8 + 5 = 13 | 13 − 8 = 5 |
| 0.8 + 0.5 = 1.3 | 1.3 − 0.8 = 0.5 |

## Practice activities

1. Each whole rod is divided into tenths. Use them to help add these.

   a)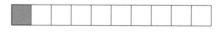

   0.5 + 0.6 = _____

   b)

   0.9 + 0.4 = _____

   c)

   0.7 + 0.7 = _____

   d)

   0.6 + 0.8 = _____

   e)

   0.5 + 0.9 = _____

   f)

   0.8 + 0.7 = _____

**2.** Use the number lines to help answer these subtractions.

**a)** ┠┼┼┼┼┼┼┼┼┼┼┼┼┼┼┼┼┨
0.2                 2.0
                  $1.8 - 0.4 =$ _____

**b)** ┠┼┼┼┼┼┼┼┼┼┨
0.6        1.7
                  $1.5 - 0.8 =$ _____

**c)** ┠┼┼┼┼┼┼┼┼┼┼┼┼┼┼┼┼┼┨
0.3                 2.1
                  $1.9 - 0.5 =$ _____

**d)** ┠┼┼┼┼┼┼┼┨
0.5      1.4
                  $1.2 - 0.7 =$ _____

**e)** ┠┼┼┼┼┼┼┼┼┼┼┼┨
0.7        1.9
                  $1.7 - 0.9 =$ _____

**f)** ┠┼┼┼┼┼┼┼┼┼┼┼┨
0.4        1.6
                  $1.4 - 0.6 =$ _____

**3.** Join each of these to the matching answer.

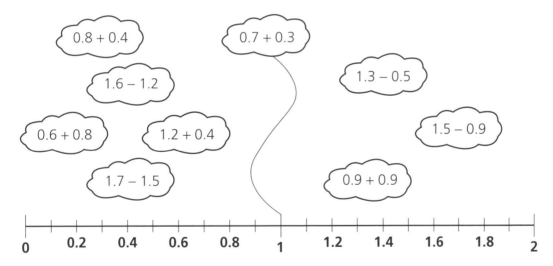

0.8 + 0.4      0.7 + 0.3      1.3 − 0.5

1.6 − 1.2

0.6 + 0.8      1.2 + 0.4      1.5 − 0.9

1.7 − 1.5      0.9 + 0.9

0   0.2   0.4   0.6   0.8   1   1.2   1.4   1.6   1.8   2

**4.** Write the missing digits, 0–5, in these calculations.

**0**    **2**    **4**

**1**    **3**    **5**

$0.8 + 0.7 = 1.\boxed{\phantom{0}}$        $1.\boxed{\phantom{0}} - 0.7 = 0.7$

$\boxed{\phantom{0}}.4 + 0.9 = 1.\boxed{\phantom{0}}$        $\boxed{\phantom{0}}.\boxed{\phantom{0}} - 0.8 = 0.4$

# Mental arithmetic test 9

**1.** Write these in order.

6.4    4.6    7.4    7.6    6.7

_____ < _____ < _____ < _____ < _____

**2.** $1.9 \times 10 =$ _____

**3.** $5.4 \div 10 =$ _____

**4.** Circle the smallest decimal number.

15.2    2.1    1.5    12.5
        1.25

**5.** Write **10** or **100** in the spaces to complete these.

$0.2 \times$ _____ $= 20$

$49.1 \times$ _____ $= 491$

**6.** Answer these.

$9 + 5 =$ _____

$0.9 + 0.5 =$ _____

**7.** $3.18 \div 10 =$ _____

**8.** Round to the nearest whole number.

5.3  $\longrightarrow$  _____

10.6  $\longrightarrow$  _____

**9.** $0.04 \times 100 =$ _____

**10.** Use the number line to answer these.

$0.7 + 0.6 =$ _____

$1.5 - 0.8 =$ _____

**11.** $67.1 \times 100 =$ _____

**12.** $132 \div 10 =$ _____

**13.** $1.7 - 0.6 =$ _____

**14.** Write these in order.

8.13    1.83    3.18    8.31    1.38

_____ < _____ < _____ < _____ < _____

**15.** $45 \div 100 =$ _____

**16.** $0.9 + 0.7 =$ _____

**17.** Round to the nearest whole number.

9.5  $\longrightarrow$  _____

12.4  $\longrightarrow$  _____

**18.** Write × or ÷ in each of these.

8.7 _____ $10 = 0.87$

8.7 _____ $10 = 87$

**19.** $5.07 \times 10 =$ _____

**20.** Write **10** or **100** in the spaces to complete these.

$94 \div$ _____ $= 9.4$

$37 \div$ _____ $= 0.37$

Score    /20

# Mental arithmetic test 10

1. Answer these.

   $4 + 7 =$ _____

   $0.4 + 0.7 =$ _____

2. Round to the nearest whole number.

   6.7 $\longrightarrow$ _____

   15.2 $\longrightarrow$ _____

3. $0.2 \times 10 =$ _____

4. Write these in order.

   2.5      7.5      2.7      5.2      7.2

   _____ < _____ < _____ < _____ < _____

5. Use the number line to answer these.

   $0.8 + 0.9 =$ _____

   $1.3 - 0.5 =$ _____

6. $57 \div 10 =$ _____

7. Write **10** or **100** in the spaces to complete these.

   $8.2 \times$ _____ $= 82$

   $0.05 \times$ _____ $= 5$

8. $4 \div 100 =$ _____

9. Circle the smallest decimal number.

   0.75      1.7      0.5      5.17

   0.57

10. Answer these.

    $14 - 9 =$ _____

    $1.4 - 0.9 =$ _____

11. $14.75 \times 100 =$ _____

12. $21.9 \div 100 =$ _____

13. Write **10** or **100** in the spaces to complete these.

    $131 \div$ _____ $= 1.31$

    $6.8 \div$ _____ $= 0.68$

14. $0.6 + 0.8 =$ _____

15. Round to the nearest whole number.

    4.8 $\longrightarrow$ _____

    11.5 $\longrightarrow$ _____

16. $1.1 - 0.3 =$ _____

17. $60.9 \times 10 =$ _____

18. Write these in order.

    10.1      90.1      99.1      90.9      10.9

    _____ < _____ < _____ < _____ < _____

19. $0.6 \div 10 =$ _____

20. Write × or ÷ in each of these.

    $14.3$ _____ $10 = 143$

    $14.3$ _____ $10 = 1.43$

**Score** /20

43

# Measures

## Learn and revise

You measure the length of objects in millimetres (mm), centimetres (cm), metres (m) and kilometres (km).

10 mm = 1 cm

100 cm = 1 m

1000 m = 1 km

You measure the capacity of containers in millilitres (ml) and litres (l).

1000 ml = 1 l

You measure the mass or weight of an object in grams (g) and kilograms (kg).

1000 g = 1 kg

You may often use decimals when measuring. For example, you can measure lengths using a mixture of centimetres and metres.

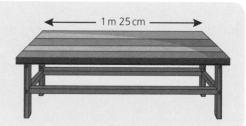

This table is 1 metre 25 centimetres long.

1 m 25 cm = 1.25 m = 125 cm

The decimal point separates the centimetres from the metres.

Lengths under 1 m can still be written as decimals, e.g. 32 cm is written as 0.32 m.

## Practice activities

1. Write the equivalent measures.

a) 55 cm = ____ m

b) $3\frac{1}{2}$ kg = _____ g

c) 3.5 l = _____ ml

d) 1.28 m = ____ cm

e) 4200 ml = ____ l ____ ml

f) 2450 g = ____ kg ____ g

g) 8 km = _____ m

h) 75 mm = ____ cm ____ mm

i) 320 cm = ____ m

j) 2000 m = ____ km

**2.** Write < , > or = to make each of these true.

**a)** 1.86 m _____ 1 m 68 cm

**b)** 1 m 10 cm _____ 110 cm

**c)** 472 cm _____ 2.74 m

**d)** 3 m 9 cm _____ 3.9 m

**e)** 835 cm _____ 8 m 35 cm

**f)** 1.06 m _____ 160 cm

**g)** 5.81 m _____ 1 m 85 cm

**h)** 46 cm _____ 0.42 m

**3.** Complete these, changing each decimal to the nearest whole number.

**a)**

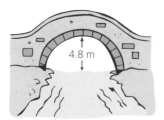

4.8 m

This bridge is approximately _____ m high.

**b)**

FLOUR

3.4 kg

This sack of flour weighs approximately _____ kg.

**c)**

5.5 litres

This bucket holds approximately _____ litres of water.

**d)**

Leeds

17.2 miles

It is approximately _____ miles to Leeds.

**e)**

63 kg  64 kg  65 kg

This woman weighs approximately _____ kg.

**f)**

4.5 m

This car is approximately _____ m long.

**4.** James uses a 3.5-litre jug and a 2.5-litre jug to fill a fish tank that holds 19 litres. He works out that he can use a mixture of full jugs to make the exact total of 19 litres.

If James uses two 2.5-litre jugs, how many 3.5-litre jugs will he need to fill the tank?

3.5 litres
3 litres
2.5 litres
2 litres
1.5 litres
1 litre
500ml

2.5 litres
2 litres
1.5 litres
1 litre
500ml

_____

# Money

## Learn and revise

These are the coins we use:

There are 100 pence in £1.

£1 = 100p

We use a decimal point to separate pounds and pence:

£1.25 = 125p or £1 and 25p

£2.30 = 230p or £2 and 30p

## Practice activities

**1.** How much money is in each purse?

a) £_____

b) £_____

c) £_____

d) £_____

**2.** Find the total of each pair of prices.

a)
| £3.50 | £1.10 |

_____

b)
| £0.40 | £1.30 |

_____

c)
| £1.70 | £2.20 |

_____

d)
| £1.10 | £3.70 |

_____

e)
| £0.60 | £0.50 |

_____

f)
| £0.80 | £0.70 |

_____

**3.** Write the change from £2 for each of these.

**a)** £2 → £1.80

Change: _____

**b)** £2 → £1.30

Change: _____

**c)** £2 → £1.95

Change: _____

**d)** £2 → £1.75

Change: _____

**e)** £2 → £0.90

Change: _____

**f)** £2 → £1.05

Change: _____

**4.** Ice-creams cost 50p each and ice-lollies cost 20p each. Amir buys some for his friends. Complete this chart to show the cost of buying different amounts. Look for patterns in the totals.

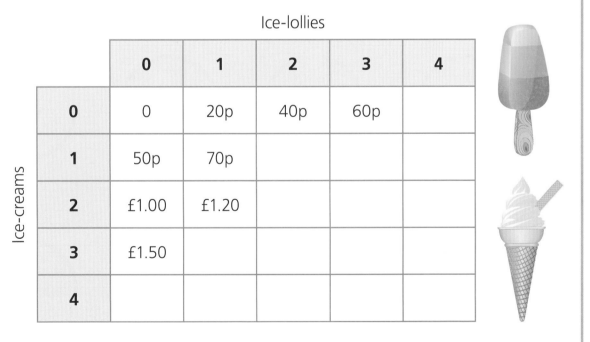

Ice-lollies

| | 0 | 1 | 2 | 3 | 4 |
|---|---|---|---|---|---|
| **0** | 0 | 20p | 40p | 60p | |
| **1** | 50p | 70p | | | |
| **2** | £1.00 | £1.20 | | | |
| **3** | £1.50 | | | | |
| **4** | | | | | |

Ice-creams

If Amir spends £2.30 in total, how many of each does he buy?

_____ ice-creams        _____ ice-lollies

# Time

## Learn and revise

There are 60 minutes in one hour.

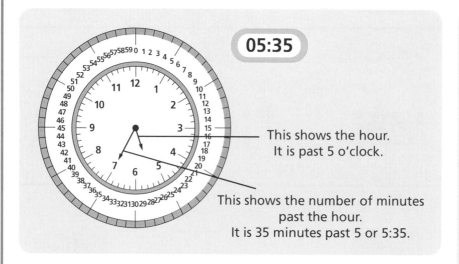

05:35

This shows the hour.
It is past 5 o'clock.

This shows the number of minutes past the hour.
It is 35 minutes past 5 or 5:35.

a.m. (ante meridiem) means before midday, so morning times.
p.m. (post meridiem) means after midday, so afternoon and evening times.

This clock shows 37 minutes past 5, or 5:37.

To read this, count on two more minutes past 5:35.

## Practice activities

1. Write the times shown on each clock face.

a)

____:____

b)

____:____

c)

____:____

d)

____:____

e)

____:____

f)

____:____

g)

____:____

h)

____:____

48

**2.** Draw these times on the clock faces. Write whether they are morning, afternoon or evening.

**a)** 2.07 p.m.

_____

**b)** 7.18 a.m.

_____

**c)** 9.12 a.m.

_____

**d)** 8.26 p.m.

_____

**e)** 3.54 p.m.

_____

**f)** 9.04 p.m.

_____

**3.** Write the time that is:

**a)** 25 minutes later than 8.50 a.m. _____

**b)** 20 minutes earlier than 11.50 a.m. _____

**c)** 45 minutes earlier than 5.20 p.m. _____

**d)** 1 hour 10 minutes later than 7.45 p.m. _____

**e)** 1 hour 35 minutes later than 10.50 a.m. _____

**f)** 2 hours 5 minutes earlier than 2.40 p.m. _____

**4.** Complete these.

**a)** 300 seconds = \_\_\_\_ minutes

**b)** 4 weeks = \_\_\_\_ days

**c)** $2\frac{1}{2}$ minutes = \_\_\_\_ seconds

**d)** $4\frac{1}{2}$ hours = \_\_\_\_ minutes

**e)** $3\frac{1}{2}$ years = \_\_\_\_ months

**f)** 56 days = \_\_\_\_ weeks

**g)** 240 hours = \_\_\_\_ days

**h)** 120 minutes = \_\_\_\_ hours

**i)** $\frac{1}{2}$ hour = \_\_\_\_ seconds

**j)** 1 week = \_\_\_\_ hours

# Mental arithmetic test 11

**1.** 4810 g = _____ kg _____ g

**2.** 85 cm = _____ mm

**3.** What is 5.4 kg rounded to the nearest whole number?

_____ kg

**4.** 1.6 litres = _____ ml

**5.** Write the time shown on each clock.

_____ a.m.        _____ p.m.

**6.** 7 km = _____ m

**7.** An adult ticket costs £1.80 and a child's ticket is 90p. How much change will you get from £3 if you buy one adult ticket and one child's ticket?

_____

**8.** 3 hours = _____ minutes

**9.** 15.3 m = _____ cm

**10.** Write <, > or = to make these true.

142 cm _____ 14 m

180 mm _____ 18 cm

**11.** Write the total amount.

£ _____

**12.** 300 cm = _____ m

**13.** What is the time 1 hour 15 minutes later than 2.30 p.m.?

_____

**14.** $7\frac{1}{2}$ kg = _____ g

**15.** When is 6.15 a.m.? Underline the answer.

morning        afternoon        evening

**16.** What is the total of 80p and £3.45?

£ _____

**17.** Round these to the nearest whole number.

24.3 l        ⟶        _____ l

0.7 km        ⟶        _____ km

**18.** 2 days = _____ hours

**19.** Sam's dentist appointment is at 11.36 a.m. He is 10 minutes late. What time does he arrive?

_____

**20.** What change will be given from £5 if you spend £3.25?

£ _____

Score        /20

50

# Mental arithmetic test 12

1. Round these to the nearest whole number.

   9.5 kg ⟶ _____ kg

   12.9 m ⟶ _____ m

2. Write the total amount.

   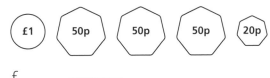

   £ _____

3. $4\frac{1}{5}$ litres = _____ ml

4. 850 cm = _____ m

5. What is the time 35 minutes later than 5.10 p.m.?

   _____

6. Add together 75p and £2.60.

   £ _____

7. 1.3 kg = _____ g

8. Write <, > or = to make these true.

   750 mm _____ 7 cm 5 mm

   63 cm _____ 6.3 m

9. When is 8.30 p.m.? Underline the answer.

   morning        afternoon        evening

10. A race is five laps of a 400 m running track. What is the length of the race in kilometres?

    _____ km

11. 4700 ml = _____ l _____ ml

12. What change will you get from £5 if you spend £1.20?

    £ _____

13. Write the time shown on each clock.

    _____ a.m.        _____ p.m.

14. 3 years = _____ months

15. What is 11.8 km rounded to the nearest whole number?

    _____ km

16. 600 seconds = _____ minutes

17. Circle the longest length.

    210 m                    1.2 km
    2100 cm
                  120 mm

18. Kate buys a drink for £1.10 and a sandwich for £1.40. How much change will she get from £3?

    _____

19. 3 weeks = _____ days

20. 8250 g = _____ kg _____ g

Score        /20

51

# Speed test

- How many of these can you complete correctly in one minute?
- Write your answers on paper. Number them 1 to 40.
- Don't worry if you cannot answer them all, just answer them as quickly as you can.
- Stop after one minute, check your answers and record your score on the progress chart opposite.
- Then, try again at another time to see if you can improve your score!

## Addition and subtraction

1. 12 − 7    = _____
2. 9 + 8     = _____
3. 13 + 6    = _____
4. 19 − 5    = _____
5. 60 + 60   = _____
6. 70 − 30   = _____
7. 7 + 8     = _____
8. 19 + 2    = _____
9. 17 − 4    = _____
10. 100 − 30 = _____
11. 14 − 5   = _____
12. 80 + 20  = _____
13. 15 − 6   = _____
14. 70 + 20  = _____
15. 16 + 5   = _____
16. 51 − 3   = _____
17. 8 + 6    = _____
18. 90 − 40  = _____
19. 18 − 9   = _____
20. 7 + 7    = _____

21. 14 + 6  = _____
22. 30 + 50 = _____
23. 13 − 5  = _____
24. 11 − 8  = _____
25. 6 + 7   = _____
26. 12 − 4  = _____
27. 9 + 3   = _____
28. 16 − 8  = _____
29. 13 − 7  = _____
30. 11 − 5  = _____
31. 5 + 9   = _____
32. 7 + 4   = _____
33. 20 − 14 = _____
34. 9 + 6   = _____
35. 13 − 8  = _____
36. 8 + 5   = _____
37. 5 + 7   = _____
38. 17 − 9  = _____
39. 8 + 3   = _____
40. 11 − 4  = _____

Colour in the stars to show your correct answers.

| Attempt | 1 | 2 | 3 | 4 | 5 | 6 |
|---|---|---|---|---|---|---|
| Date | | | | | | |

**Scores out of 40**

| | 39 40 | 39 40 | 39 40 | 39 40 | 39 40 | 39 40 |
|---|---|---|---|---|---|---|
| | 37 38 | 37 38 | 37 38 | 37 38 | 37 38 | 37 38 |
| | 35 36 | 35 36 | 35 36 | 35 36 | 35 36 | 35 36 |
| | 33 34 | 33 34 | 33 34 | 33 34 | 33 34 | 33 34 |
| | 31 32 | 31 32 | 31 32 | 31 32 | 31 32 | 31 32 |
| | 29 30 | 29 30 | 29 30 | 29 30 | 29 30 | 29 30 |
| | 27 28 | 27 28 | 27 28 | 27 28 | 27 28 | 27 28 |
| | 25 26 | 25 26 | 25 26 | 25 26 | 25 26 | 25 26 |
| | 23 24 | 23 24 | 23 24 | 23 24 | 23 24 | 23 24 |
| | 21 22 | 21 22 | 21 22 | 21 22 | 21 22 | 21 22 |
| | 19 20 | 19 20 | 19 20 | 19 20 | 19 20 | 19 20 |
| | 17 18 | 17 18 | 17 18 | 17 18 | 17 18 | 17 18 |
| | 15 16 | 15 16 | 15 16 | 15 16 | 15 16 | 15 16 |
| | 13 14 | 13 14 | 13 14 | 13 14 | 13 14 | 13 14 |
| | 11 12 | 11 12 | 11 12 | 11 12 | 11 12 | 11 12 |
| | 9 10 | 9 10 | 9 10 | 9 10 | 9 10 | 9 10 |
| | 7 8 | 7 8 | 7 8 | 7 8 | 7 8 | 7 8 |
| | 5 6 | 5 6 | 5 6 | 5 6 | 5 6 | 5 6 |
| | 3 4 | 3 4 | 3 4 | 3 4 | 3 4 | 3 4 |
| | 1 2 | 1 2 | 1 2 | 1 2 | 1 2 | 1 2 |

# Speed test

- How many of these can you complete correctly in one minute?
- Write your answers on paper. Number them 1 to 40.
- Don't worry if you cannot answer them all, just answer them as quickly as you can.
- Stop after one minute, check your answers and record your score on the progress chart opposite.
- Then, try again at another time to see if you can improve your score!

## Multiplication and division

1. 6 × 7 = _____
2. 3 × 12 = _____
3. 7 × 4 = _____
4. 28 ÷ 7 = _____
5. 11 × 8 = _____
6. 6 × 5 = _____
7. 3 × 9 = _____
8. 49 ÷ 7 = _____
9. 20 ÷ 2 = _____
10. 12 × 5 = _____
11. 9 × 11 = _____
12. 8 × 8 = _____
13. 77 ÷ 7 = _____
14. 12 ÷ 4 = _____
15. 3 × 7 = _____
16. 5 × 5 = _____
17. 9 × 8 = _____
18. 45 ÷ 5 = _____
19. 56 ÷ 8 = _____
20. 5 × 3 = _____

21. 60 ÷ 10 = _____
22. 6 × 9 = _____
23. 42 ÷ 7 = _____
24. 35 ÷ 7 = _____
25. 3 × 3 = _____
26. 6 × 2 = _____
27. 4 × 9 = _____
28. 27 ÷ 3 = _____
29. 36 ÷ 6 = _____
30. 28 ÷ 4 = _____
31. 8 × 5 = _____
32. 4 × 0 = _____
33. 7 × 2 = _____
34. 48 ÷ 8 = _____
35. 12 × 7 = _____
36. 4 × 12 = _____
37. 27 ÷ 9 = _____
38. 32 ÷ 4 = _____
39. 7 × 8 = _____
40. 18 ÷ 9 = _____

# Progress chart

Colour in the stars to show your correct answers.

| Attempt | 1 | 2 | 3 | 4 | 5 | 6 |
|---|---|---|---|---|---|---|
| Date | | | | | | |

**Scores out of 40**

Rows (top to bottom):

| 39 40 | 39 40 | 39 40 | 39 40 | 39 40 | 39 40 |
| 37 38 | 37 38 | 37 38 | 37 38 | 37 38 | 37 38 |
| 35 36 | 35 36 | 35 36 | 35 36 | 35 36 | 35 36 |
| 33 34 | 33 34 | 33 34 | 33 34 | 33 34 | 33 34 |
| 31 32 | 31 32 | 31 32 | 31 32 | 31 32 | 31 32 |
| 29 30 | 29 30 | 29 30 | 29 30 | 29 30 | 29 30 |
| 27 28 | 27 28 | 27 28 | 27 28 | 27 28 | 27 28 |
| 25 26 | 25 26 | 25 26 | 25 26 | 25 26 | 25 26 |
| 23 24 | 23 24 | 23 24 | 23 24 | 23 24 | 23 24 |
| 21 22 | 21 22 | 21 22 | 21 22 | 21 22 | 21 22 |
| 19 20 | 19 20 | 19 20 | 19 20 | 19 20 | 19 20 |
| 17 18 | 17 18 | 17 18 | 17 18 | 17 18 | 17 18 |
| 15 16 | 15 16 | 15 16 | 15 16 | 15 16 | 15 16 |
| 13 14 | 13 14 | 13 14 | 13 14 | 13 14 | 13 14 |
| 11 12 | 11 12 | 11 12 | 11 12 | 11 12 | 11 12 |
| 9 10 | 9 10 | 9 10 | 9 10 | 9 10 | 9 10 |
| 7 8 | 7 8 | 7 8 | 7 8 | 7 8 | 7 8 |
| 5 6 | 5 6 | 5 6 | 5 6 | 5 6 | 5 6 |
| 3 4 | 3 4 | 3 4 | 3 4 | 3 4 | 3 4 |
| 1 2 | 1 2 | 1 2 | 1 2 | 1 2 | 1 2 |

# Speed test

- How many of these can you complete correctly in one minute?
- Write your answers on paper. Number them 1 to 40.
- Don't worry if you cannot answer them all, just answer them as quickly as you can.
- Stop after one minute, check your answers and record your score on the progress chart opposite.
- Then, try again at another time to see if you can improve your score!

## Mixed problems

1. $4 \times 9$ = _____
2. $7 + 7$ = _____
3. $17 - 6$ = _____
4. $45 \div 9$ = _____
5. $32 \div 4$ = _____
6. $90 + 40$ = _____
7. $80 - 50$ = _____
8. $40 + 30$ = _____
9. $8 \times 7$ = _____
10. $12 \times 5$ = _____
11. $12 - 6$ = _____
12. $190 - 70$ = _____
13. $20 \div 2$ = _____
14. $90 + 90$ = _____
15. $18 + 4$ = _____
16. $3 \times 11$ = _____
17. $6 \times 6$ = _____
18. $15 - 8$ = _____
19. $42 \div 7$ = _____
20. $24 \div 8$ = _____

21. $20 + 90$ = _____
22. $30 + 60$ = _____
23. $63 \div 9$ = _____
24. $11 - 7$ = _____
25. $3 \times 5$ = _____
26. $8 \times 8$ = _____
27. $9 + 8$ = _____
28. $14 - 9$ = _____
29. $15 - 7$ = _____
30. $35 \div 7$ = _____
31. $44 \div 4$ = _____
32. $34 + 6$ = _____
33. $50 + 70$ = _____
34. $12 - 3$ = _____
35. $16 - 9$ = _____
36. $4 \times 5$ = _____
37. $15 \div 3$ = _____
38. $6 \times 9$ = _____
39. $12 \times 3$ = _____
40. $8 + 8$ = _____

# Progress chart

Colour in the stars to show your correct answers.

| Attempt | 1 | 2 | 3 | 4 | 5 | 6 |
|---------|---|---|---|---|---|---|
| Date | | | | | | |

**Scores out of 40**

# Key facts

| Thousands | Hundreds | Tens | Ones |
|---|---|---|---|
| 4 | 7 | 3 | 8 |

**4000** ⟩ **700** ⟩ **30** ⟩ **8** ⟩

4738 = 4000 + 700 + 30 + 8

four thousand seven hundred and thirty-eight

## Fractions and decimals

| $\frac{1}{2} = 0.5$ | $\frac{1}{4} = 0.25$ | $\frac{3}{4} = 0.75$ |
|---|---|---|
| $\frac{1}{5} = 0.2$ | $\frac{1}{10} = 0.1$ | $\frac{2}{5} = 0.4$ |

## Multiplication and division

| × | 1 | 2 | 3 | 4 | 5 | 6 | 7 | 8 | 9 | 10 | 11 | 12 |
|---|---|---|---|---|---|---|---|---|---|---|---|---|
| **1** | 1 | 2 | 3 | 4 | 5 | 6 | 7 | 8 | 9 | 10 | 11 | 12 |
| **2** | 2 | 4 | 6 | 8 | 10 | 12 | 14 | 16 | 18 | 20 | 22 | 24 |
| **3** | 3 | 6 | 9 | 12 | 15 | 18 | 21 | 24 | 27 | 30 | 33 | 36 |
| **4** | 4 | 8 | 12 | 16 | 20 | 24 | 28 | 32 | 36 | 40 | 44 | 48 |
| **5** | 5 | 10 | 15 | 20 | 25 | 30 | 35 | 40 | 45 | 50 | 55 | 60 |
| **6** | 6 | 12 | 18 | 24 | 30 | 36 | 42 | 48 | 54 | 60 | 66 | 72 |
| **7** | 7 | 14 | 21 | 28 | 35 | 42 | 49 | 56 | 63 | 70 | 77 | 84 |
| **8** | 8 | 16 | 24 | 32 | 40 | 48 | 56 | 64 | 72 | 80 | 88 | 96 |
| **9** | 9 | 18 | 27 | 36 | 45 | 54 | 63 | 72 | 81 | 90 | 99 | 108 |
| **10** | 10 | 20 | 30 | 40 | 50 | 60 | 70 | 80 | 90 | 100 | 110 | 120 |
| **11** | 11 | 22 | 33 | 44 | 55 | 66 | 77 | 88 | 99 | 110 | 121 | 132 |
| **12** | 12 | 24 | 36 | 48 | 60 | 72 | 84 | 96 | 108 | 120 | 132 | 144 |

## Addition and subtraction

| + | 1 | 2 | 3 | 4 | 5 | 6 | 7 | 8 | 9 | 10 |
|----|----|----|----|----|----|----|----|----|----|----|
| 1 | 2 | 3 | 4 | 5 | 6 | 7 | 8 | 9 | 10 | 11 |
| 2 | 3 | 4 | 5 | 6 | 7 | 8 | 9 | 10 | 11 | 12 |
| 3 | 4 | 5 | 6 | 7 | 8 | 9 | 10 | 11 | 12 | 13 |
| 4 | 5 | 6 | 7 | 8 | 9 | 10 | 11 | 12 | 13 | 14 |
| 5 | 6 | 7 | 8 | 9 | 10 | 11 | 12 | 13 | 14 | 15 |
| 6 | 7 | 8 | 9 | 10 | 11 | 12 | 13 | 14 | 15 | 16 |
| 7 | 8 | 9 | 10 | 11 | 12 | 13 | 14 | 15 | 16 | 17 |
| 8 | 9 | 10 | 11 | 12 | 13 | 14 | 15 | 16 | 17 | 18 |
| 9 | 10 | 11 | 12 | 13 | 14 | 15 | 16 | 17 | 18 | 19 |
| 10 | 11 | 12 | 13 | 14 | 15 | 16 | 17 | 18 | 19 | 20 |

## Measures

| Length | Capacity | Weight/mass |
|--------|----------|-------------|
| 1 kilometre (km) = 1000 metres (m)<br>1 metre (m) = 100 centimetres (cm)<br>1 centimetre (cm) = 10 millimetres (mm) | 1 litre (l) = 1000 millilitres (ml) | 1 kilogram (kg) = 1000 grams (g) |

## Time

1 minute = 60 seconds

1 hour = 60 minutes

1 day = 24 hours

1 week = 7 days

1 fortnight = 14 days

1 year = 12 months = 365 days

leap year = 366 days

10:00 10:05 10:10 10:15 10:20 10:25

10:30 10:35 10:40 10:45 10:50 10:55

# Acknowledgements

The author and publisher are grateful to the copyright holders for permission to use quoted materials and images.

Cover, P01 ©Igorrita; P09 ©Klara Viskova; P17 ©Suerz; P24 ©Casejustin; P25 ©Skalapendra; P31 ©Sergey Mat; P44 ©Matthew Cole; P45 ©Alegria; P45 ©i3alda; P52, 54, 56 ©Elmm

The above images have been used under license from Shutterstock.com

All other images are © Letts Educational, an imprint of HarperCollins*Publishers* Ltd

Every effort has been made to trace copyright holders and obtain their permission for the use of copyright material. The author and publisher will gladly receive information enabling them to rectify any error or omission in subsequent editions. All facts are correct at time of going to press.

Published by Letts Educational
An imprint of HarperCollins*Publishers* Ltd
1 London Bridge Street
London SE1 9GF

ISBN 9780008294120

First published 2013

This edition published 2018

10 9 8 7 6 5 4 3 2

Text © 2018 Paul Broadbent

Design © 2018 Letts Educational, an imprint of HarperCollins*Publishers* Ltd

British Library Cataloguing in Publication Data.

A CIP record of this book is available from the British Library.

Commissioning Editor: Tammy Poggo

Author: Paul Broadbent

Project Manager: Richard Toms

Editorial: Amanda Dickson and Richard Toms

Cover Design: Paul Oates

Inside Concept Design: Ian Wrigley

Layout: Jouve India Private Limited

Production: Natalia Rebow

Printed and bound by
Martins the Printers, Berwick upon Tweed

**MIX**
Paper from
responsible source
**FSC** www.fsc.org **FSC C007454**

This book is produced from independently certified FSC™ paper to ensure responsible forest management.

For more information visit:
www.harpercollins.co.uk/green